MODALITIES IN MEDIEVAL JEWISH LAW
FOR PUBLIC ORDER AND SAFETY

HEBREW UNION COLLEGE ANNUAL SUPPLEMENTS

NUMBER SIX

Modalities in Medieval Jewish Law for Public Order and Safety

Stephen M. Passamaneck

CINCINNATI 2009

The publication of this volume
of the Hebrew Union College Annual
was subventioned by

The Henry Englander-Eli Mayer Publication Fund
established in their honor by
Esther Straus Englander and Jessie Straus Mayer

LIBRARY OF CONGRESS CATALOGING-IN-PUBLICATION DATA

Passamaneck, Stephen M.
Modalities in Medieval Jewish Law for Public Order and Safety
p. cm. — (Hebrew Union College Annual. Supplements; no. 6)
Includes bibliographical references.

ISBN 978-0-87820-605-6 (alk. paper)

1. Criminal law (Jewish law) — History — To 1500. I. Title.

KBM3800.P37 2009
340.5'8–DC22   2009012462

Design and composition by Kelby Bowers
Printed in the United States of America

For Connie
Her memory is an enduring blessing.

. . . R. Yaʾakov bar Idi said that R. Yoḥanan said, One may
attend to matters of life and death urgency
and of communal urgency on the Sabbath and attend
Synagogues in order to deal with public matters
on the Sabbath . . . .

Babylonian Talmud Tractate *Šabbat* 150a

Submissions

We welcome for consideration scholarly essays in Jewish and Cognate Studies, Ancient and Modern: Bible, Rabbinics, Language and Literature, History, Philosophy, Religion. Please address your submission inquiries to The Editor at *annual@huc.edu*.

Authors submitting manuscripts for publication are asked to do the following:

1 For manuscript formatting, follow *The University of Chicago Manual of Style* in general and *The SBL Handbook of Style* specifically.
2 All manuscripts, including notes, should be continuously paginated, double-spaced and employ generous margins all around.
3 Every manuscript must include an English abstract of 200 words maximum.
4 Submissions should be sent in Portable Document Format (PDF) as email attachments to *annual@huc.edu*.

Previous Volumes

The *Annual* office can supply vols. XLV–LXXVI excluding vol. LV (out of stock): vols. XLV–LII at $15.00, vols. LIII–LVIII at $20.00, vols. LIX–LXXII at $30.00, and vols. LXXIII–LXXVI at $40.00. Printed copies of individual articles are available for a fee of $5.00. For more information email the *Annual* office at: *annual@huc.edu*. The American Jewish Periodicals Center at HUC-JIR, 3101 Clifton Avenue, Cincinnati, Ohio 45220 can supply microfilm copies of vols. XXXVIII–XLIV. ProQuest Company, 300 North Zeeb Road, Ann Arbor, Michigan 48106 can supply 16 mm, 35 mm, 105 mm microfiche, as well as photocopies.

Supplements

Yosef Hayim Yerushalmi. *The Lisbon Massacre of 1506 and the Royal Image in the Shebet Yehudah*. 1976.

Mark E. Cohen. *Sumerian Hymnology: the* Eršemma. 1981.

William C. Gwaltney, Jr. *The Pennsylvania Old Assyrian Texts*. 1982.

Kenneth R. Stow. *"The 1007 Anonymous" and Papal Sovereignty. Jewish Perceptions of the Papacy and Papal Policy in the High Middle Ages*. 1985.

Martin A. Cohen. *The Canonization of a Myth: Portugal's "Jewish Problem" and the Assembly of Tomar 1629*. 2002.

Stephen M. Passamaneck. *Modalities in Medieval Jewish Law for Public Order and Safety*. 2009.

Hebrew Union College Annual
3101 Clifton Avenue, Cincinnati, Ohio 45220

Contents

Acknowledgments

I acknowledge with sincere thanks three men whose comments and criticisms have strengthened this work: my colleague Prof. Joshua Holo, Rabbi Dr. Walter Jacob, and Daniel Passamaneck, Esq. Any remaining faults, whether of omission or commission are mine alone. I also wish to acknowledge with gratitude the work of Ms. Amy Morrison, who labored long and lovingly over the typescript.

Introduction

The history of medieval Jewry presents one inescapable fact: the Jews were a people apart. No matter where or when we find a Jewish community in the Middle Ages, it was an "alien" enclave in a host society which was sometimes cordial to it and sometimes not.[1] Jews were a foreign element which managed its own communal affairs, creating religious, educational and charitable institutions, mechanisms for collection and disbursement of taxes to the host government, and various systems for internal governance and the administration of justice. The Jews governed themselves and dispensed justice in so far as possible according to the *halakhah*, their ancient internal legal system.[2] This legal system was the subject of devoted and loving study and careful enhancement over the centuries by skillful interpretation, by mixture of local customs and by local ordinances, which helped the system keep pace with changing circumstances. Presently there will be more to say on the sense in which the general term *halakhah*, Jewish law, is used here.

In the discussion of the administration of justice in medieval Jewish communities, one area of concern is probably assumed to be present, yet it has been obscured by its diffusion among treatments of various other topics falling under the general heading of communal organization and powers, for example, taxation and criminal law. This is the specific area of maintaining public safety and public order. This subject is a matter, however, upon which everything else in civil society really rests, and it is clearly of utmost concern to a people living as an alien element within an ever watchful host community. Indeed no host society would suffer a minority group that would not or could not maintain themselves in a peaceful and orderly fashion that satisfied the expectations of the majority community. Since the Jews perceived themselves and were perceived by others as a separate (and special) nation, they did not want any host government mixing into internal Jewish governance. Therefore, it behooved the Jews to set and maintain a standard of internal peace and order that did not require implicit or explicit involvement of the host government. Some exceptional circumstances arose in which Jews did require host assistance, but the dominant attitude appears to have been to keep internal matters in Jewish hands. The hosts after all could rob and expel the Jews at will if the Jews did not meet

---

1 The term alien, set off in quotation marks here, underscores the fact that the Jews were simply "other," the basic meaning of alien. It has nothing to do with foreignness since the Jews of a particular area might have lived there for generations. No matter: Jews were the "other" either despised for their faith or a tolerated sub-class.

2 The extent to which the Jews could control matters of internal safety and order will become clear in the course of this essay.

9

the expectations of the government. Internal peace and order were always in the Jews' very best interest.

Although the Talmud refers to "needs of the people" (*tsorke rabbim*) and "public emergencies" (*piquah rabbim*), these terms do not rise to the level of a separate rubric comprising public order and public safety as such in the *halakhah*, *piquah rabbim* being very rare indeed. The absence of such a discrete category in medieval rabbinic writing should therefore cause no surprise since the various subheadings of *halakhah* closely adhere to the ancient nomenclature of the Mishnah and the Gemara.

Public order and public safety involve the realities of power. Various Jewish communities in medieval Spain, particularly in Castile, enjoyed the broadest such powers, including from time to time and place to place, jurisdiction in capital cases.[3] Yet all Jewish communities possessed some degree of authority to maintain internal peace and order. The cases to be reviewed here are not, however, limited to material from medieval Spain.

As has been noted, Jewish communities used their own internal legal system, *halakhah*. The Jewish law in our own day is often understood as benign and substantially in conformity with modern western ethical ideals. *Halakhah* requires us to care for the poor, the sick, the orphan, to do justice and eschew fraud and falsehood. All that is so, but the realities of power bring another aspect of Jewish law to the forefront. The modalities for maintenance of peace and order were often harsh and extremely cruel compared to the legal standards of today. The medieval authorities were of course very well aware of the high ethical principles embedded in the *halakhah*, but the tasks of governance and the maintenance of peace and order also made other demands: there were realities that had to be faced and problems that had to be resolved. How the medieval authorities, however, dealt with these realities is as much a part of the

---

3 The secondary sources on medieval Jewry are myriad. Some of the classic works that touch upon the matters addressed here are Yitzhak Baer, *A History of the Jews in Christian Spain*, trans. Louis Schoffman (2 vols.; Philadelphia: Jewish Publication Society of America, 1961–66) (trans. from the Heb.); Shlomo Eidelberg, *Jewish Life in Austria in the XV Century* (Philadelphia: Dropsie College, 1962); Isidore Epstein, *The Responsa of R. Solomon b. Adret* (New York: KTAV, 1968); Louis Finkelstein, *Jewish Self Government in the Middle Ages* (New York: Feldman Publishing Co., 1964); Abraham Hershman, *Rabbi Isaac b. Sheshet Perfet and His Times* (New York: Jewish Theological Seminary of America, 1943); Aaron Kirschenbaum, *Self-Incrimination in Jewish Law* (New York: Burning Bush Press, 1970); Abraham A. Neuman, *The Jews in Spain* (Philadelphia: The Jewish Publication Society of America, 1942); Emanuel Quint and Neil S. Hecht, *Jewish Jurisprudence* (2 vols.; Chur, Switzerland: Harwood Academic Pub., 1980–86); the articles and essays on the matter form a considerable library in themselves. Though somewhat out of date, Prof. Nahum Rakover's *Multi-Language Bibliography of Jewish Law* (Jerusalem: Library of Jewish Law, 1990) is extremely useful. Public order and safety do not appear as subheadings in any of these works.

Jewish tradition as the ethical and moral idealism they also espoused in other contexts. Modern fashion may be more inclined to overlook these difficult problems of power or to mask them utterly and speak of the ethical high road as if it were the whole of the matter; this is vaguely dishonest. It is also a misreading of history. Dismissing some of the material that is presented especially in the punitive modality section as a series of medieval horror stories does not reckon with its origin and context. This material comes from the most distinguished and respected Rabbis of their age. Beside their learning and piety which no one questions they also possessed power and authority. They were towers of rabbinic authority, and their writ ran in Jewish communities with a force that the rabbinate anywhere has not wielded for generations.

Their decisions and suggestions do not by any means represent a present day view of the application of Jewish ideals and ethics to modern problems in public order and public safety. Certainly I do not present any brief that they should. Nevertheless they do demonstrate, as we shall presently observe, an aspect of Jewish law that is as real and as authentic as any other. Men with power take strong action, and that is as true of our rabbinic ancestors as it is of any other group. We are well advised not to suffer an amnesia in this regard. People who govern and guide and exercise real power simply have to make certain kinds of decisions according to their lights, whether we might applaud them or not in our own day, from our present point of view. Indeed, modern Jewish leadership, whether rabbinic or lay, does not and cannot exercise power in the fields of public safety and order as a regular aspect of their duties: they do not suppress or investigate crime, adjudicate criminal matters or fight fires.

This essay does not by any means suggest that medieval Jewry had a significant element of ruffians and lawbreakers. That is surely not so. But there were some who did disturb the peace of the community, and even a small number of such persons could seriously upset the tenor of life, particularly in the rather small (by modern standards) Jewish settlements in medieval Europe. Such communities did not have the anonymity of tens or hundreds of thousands of people living over a large area; medieval towns were small and quite cramped, even the largest of them. Further, the Jews of those bygone centuries were people of vigor and passion, fully possessed of the entire range of human strengths and weaknesses. The very precariousness of Jewish life as an alien element in a host society arguably enhanced the possibility of friction among Jews — as well as their need for internal solidarity and cohesion. It is not pleasant perhaps to contemplate disrupters of the public peace, but neither is it proper to ignore them as though such people never existed.

The expression "public order" as it is used here is in its broadest sense an aspect of maintaining the social (and political) balance between the host society and the Jewish community. The present interest focuses on the internal peace and order of the Jews themselves. There are various components of public order as it appears here. One element of public order is an atmosphere of general harmony among the families and individuals who comprise community. A private quarrel surely had the potential of blossoming into a public cause célèbre that could divide a community.[4] A premium was put on peaceful interpersonal relations. The second element is an atmosphere of stability which allows the economic activity of the people to proceed smoothly and maintains a respect towards the people and institutions of the host society. The final element, and perhaps the most important one, may be termed a general respect for and adherence to Jewish law and Jewish usage that pervade both the public and the private life of the community, and allow the well-known and necessary institutions of Jewish life (the synagogue, the *bet din, baté midrash*, charities, the *miqweh* and so forth) to serve the needs of the people without quarrel or disruption. When these elements are present, a sense of public order (and public safety) obtains. Public order is a complicated phenomenon, involving the protection of individuals and institutions. Thus when the expressions "public order" and "public safety" are used here they imply the presence of all three elements.

Matters of public order and public safety we encounter in modern life, more often than not, fall into the area of criminal law. That is also the perspective that the *halakhah* has toward them. The primary concern is with acts, threats or situations that pose an immediate danger to persons, the public weal or are *per se* repugnant to the community's moral sense.

Since the area of criminal law is so closely related to public order and public safety, a comment on criminal law in the *halakhah* is a necessary preliminary exposition. First, it is to be understood that the origins and development of the *halakhah* are not here in point. How, where, when, and why it emerged from biblical and early rabbinic materials as it did has no bearing on the sense of the term, since by the Middle Ages, the Rabbis and the lay leadership of Jewish communities looked back upon the laws of the Talmud and the generations of post-talmudic legal development as presenting a fully formed, comprehensive legal system dating back to the earliest days of the Jewish people. The medieval rabbis inherited the legal tradition as their internal legal system, which by their lights had always been the legal system for the Jews from Sinai on to whatever extent the outside world had allowed it to operate as such.

Further, with respect to criminal law the *halakhah* presents a system whose apparent purpose is indeed the maintenance of public order and public safety,

---

4 See Appendix 1 for an event that could have easily split a community if indeed it did not in fact do so. Other matters that will be reviewed here surely marshaled partisans to the respective sides even though those communal reverberations were really no part of the determination and imposition of the appropriate modality.

yet it turns out to be quite unlike that of western legal systems. The categories of "criminal" law and "civil" law are not really relevant in Jewish law. First the concept of "criminal law" implies an offense against the sovereign or the state. Since Jewish law is, classically, a matter of divine revelation, any offense, even one against the "rabbinic" rules, that is, those promulgated by "the Rabbis," as apposed to the biblical rules, may ultimately be conceived as an offense against the Divine. It is therefore best to eschew the categories imported from other legal systems and allow Jewish law to be understood through its own categories.

The *halakhah* recognizes two main areas, each of which includes matters that western law considers criminal offenses. One, *diné nefashot*, covers what the Rabbis considered the classic capital crimes: cases of *nefashot*; cases involving lives. The specifications and procedures of the *diné nefashot* appear in the *mishnah* (and *gemara*) of the talmudic tractate *Sanhedrin*. I term these rules the "classic rules" for they are indeed the "classic" statement of the laws, as understood by later generations governing the specifications of the various wrongful acts deemed capital matters, evidence, modes of execution, composition of the competent courts, and related matters. The wrongful acts include, *inter alia*, willful homicide, a number of sexual offenses of an incestuous nature, the adultery of a married woman, and idolatry.[5] In modern western criminal law, willful homicide may carry a capital penalty though many jurisdictions have rejected it in recent years. The sexual offenses may be criminal acts, but they are not capital crimes in western law though some non-western systems do punish various sexual offenses capitally. Modern western law is not concerned with idolatry, which it would deem a wholly ecclesiastical matter.

A second category of cases is the *diné mammonot*, cases of money and property, pecuniary matters. These include many offenses which are deemed criminal in modern western law: mayhem, robbery, rape, battery and burglary. The *halakhah* punishes these offenses by means of various fines, mulcts, and payment of damages, so they are "pecuniary" cases in a Jewish light and tried by a court of three, not twenty-three, as in capital matters. Because the punishments are expressed in pecuniary terms, they are often called "civil" cases even though an armed robbery is clearly different from a landlord-tenant dispute. The resolution of mayhem and battery cases also involves the seeking and granting pardon as between the offender and his victim.

We move now to a more detailed examination of *diné nefashot*, which is relevant in matters of public order and safety. Consideration of *diné mammonot* will occur later.

As I have noted, the classic Jewish criminal code on *diné nefashot* appears in the *mishnah* of tractate *Sanhedrin*. This material, along with the intense

5 See *m.Sanh.* 7:4, 9:1.

examination and discussion of it in the *gemara* of *Sanhedrin,* was amplified
by centuries of rabbinic commentary, "case law," and codification with further
commentary.[6] It has also received a significant volume of critical scholarly attention for over a century and a half.

Most recently, Beth Berkowitz has carefully catalogued and described this
scholarly output, but only two of the legions of scholars whom she mentioned as
a contributor to the list of works analyzing and reanalyzing the rabbinic criminal code come close to a consideration of public order and public safety: Arnold
Enker and Aaron Kirschenbaum.[7] Kirschenbaum relies heavily on a sermon
of the fourteenth-century master R. Nissim Gerondi. Kirschenbaum argues that
the rabbis of the Talmud, and their medieval successors, regarded the criminal
law of the Torah as primarily a mighty instrument of character training, religious indoctrination and spiritual edification, and only secondarily (and sometimes not at all) of practical import. The unlovely details of day to day criminal
justice fell into the province of royal law in theory exercised by Jewish, including of course Davidic, kings. This royal law dealt with peace and order. They
also appear in the area of rabbinic exigency jurisdiction, which will figure significantly in this inquiry. In reality, however, the possibility of a Jewish king who
would be responsible for the maintenance of peace and order in society was as
much a pious wish and hope for medieval Jewry as was the reconstitution of
the Sanhedrin in the Hall of Hewn Stone. This leaves only the exigency jurisdiction to attend to the daily requirements of society. Although Kirschenbaum
discusses exigency jurisdiction, he does not explore the obvious fact that of all
the elements of the criminal code (classic rules, the Jewish King, the heavenly
tribunal, and exigency jurisdiction), only the last really functioned as a means
of attaining a measure of criminal justice within Jewish communities. The
religious-spiritual educational purposes which Kirschenbaum sees as the principal purpose of the classic Jewish criminal code, "overrides and overshadows
its societal function of . . . supervising law and order." A serious implication of
this vision of the law will presently be examined.

While fully acknowledging the spiritual and educational functions of the Jewish criminal law, one must still face a very real and practical question. Our medieval ancestors did not live their lives wholly in the synagogue and the house
of study. Public safety and public order were obviously daily concerns. The

6   The "case law" is the *responsa* literature. On this see Solomon Freehof, *The Responsa Literature*
    (Philadelphia: The Jewish Publication Society of America, 1955). In the course of time, responsa
    cited not only Bible and Talmud, but talmudic commentary, local ordinances, other responsa
    and various restatements of the law that appeared over the centuries. The responsa became an
    extremely complex literature drawing on numerous biblical and rabbinic sources.
7   Beth A. Berkowitz, *Execution and Invention* (Oxford: Univ. Press, 2006) esp. 44–46 on Kirschen-
    baum and Enker.

community had to take these matters seriously. If the preamble of the United States Constitution is any witness on matters of governance and government, the establishment of justice and domestic tranquility rank high among the purposes of governance and the tasks of government. If the communal structures of medieval communities had not included a genuine and effective mechanism for maintenance of peace and order they simply could not have endured. They would have succumbed time after time to internal quarrels and no host society would wish to harbor such an unruly group. The intervention of the host government was an ever-present danger that no Jew wished to see. Consequences of such a take-over could hardly be benign.

The Heavenly Court, for all its majesty, and the devout yearning for a Jewish king were not enough to maintain a peaceful community. The people needed a real sense that they were not going to be at the mercy of home-grown predators. To be at the mercy of non-Jewish thugs and thieves was bad enough, but to be vulnerable to the native variety would have been intolerable, without some means of dealing with them. The classic rules were no help in this. Under the classic rules alone, society was seriously at risk, and that state of affairs was obviously unacceptable. Thus we come to the examination of the various modalities that medieval communities developed to maintain peace and order. These modalities often have ancient talmudic antecedents, and those talmudic bases will be reviewed.

Much, but by no means all, of the material we shall examine involves capital and corporal punishments, flogging, excommunication, fines, and restitution. In short, these are the various ways in which medieval Jewish authorities required the offender to pay, at times most grievously, for his or her offense. Usually one thinks of them simply as the result of the legal system taking its proper course. But a legal system is part of a larger social structure. It is not independent of that structure which relies on it for safety and protection. If we shift our perception of these punishments and penalties, we see them as more than the just (or unjust?) desserts for offenders. They become an important aspect of social control and communal structure. These punishments and penalties were also to serve as examples and lessons to the entire community. They did not occur behind prison walls where the public would hardly be aware of them. The broader perspective allows us to think of them and consider them as affecting more than the court and the offenders. Public order and public safety concerned everyone.

The most serious breaches of the public peace required the most severe penalty: capital punishment. The Jewish "criminal code" presents two diametrically opposed treatments of the matter. The classic rules in this matter are so tightly drawn that they are useless as a method for successfully prosecuting offenders. Long before anyone could have faced the executioner (or executioners) under the classic rules, the prosecution would have had to circumvent formidable obstacles which for all practical purposes could not be overcome. Let us consider briefly these obstacles.

First, apparently no provision exists for bringing an offender to court. One finds no mention of a hue and cry. No officer appears to be charged with the duty of finding and presenting the offender to the judges. It would appear that offenses we would consider "criminal" would have been treated as matters between private individuals. There is no "state" machinery to bring offenders to justice: no "public prosecutor" or even a "public" accuser. Such offices were and are unknown in Jewish law. The witnesses are quite probably themselves the accusers which would account for the intense interrogation they undergo (*m.Sanh.* 5:1–4). Any system that would apparently rely on bystanders and witnesses to seize the culprit and spirit him (or her) away to the court is already at a grave disadvantage in providing an effective criminal law. *Mishnah Sanhedrin* 7:10 refers to witnesses who bring an offender to court after setting up a situation where the person incriminated himself with respect to idolatry, but this scenario requires some planning on the part of the witnesses. It is not, as some might suppose, a case of entrapment, since the accused had clearly formed the intent to commit the act before the witnessed incrimination occurred.

Second, no confession, no matter how genuine or how sincere, may be heard under the classic rules.[8] How much the more is any coerced confession inadmissible under those rules.

Third, the case against the offender must be made by two adult male Jews of good character who are not relatives of the accused or each other, and who were positioned in reasonably close proximity to each other.[9] Women, minors, slaves, mentally defective persons, deaf-mutes, the blind, and non-Jews are all unacceptable as witnesses under the classic rules. Interested parties are excluded. Gamblers and lawbreakers are excluded. The requirement that witnesses be persons of good character and not barred as lawful witnesses for any substantive reason rather reckons without the actual circumstances of various crimes. For instance, willful (or premeditated) homicide often occurs at night when such potential witnesses are home in bed; or it happens in out of the way places specifically chosen for their privacy. Incest is hardly likely to occur where qualified witnesses are available, and the same holds true for the adultery of a married woman. Homicide is probably going to occur more frequently among those who are already lawbreakers or gamblers or others whose conduct marks them as unfit to give testimony. The problem of qualified witnesses alone renders conviction a virtual impossibility.

---

8 See Aaron Kirschenbaum, *Self-Incrimination in Jewish Law* (New York: Burning Bush Press, 1970). This masterful work covers the matter comprehensively.

9 *m.Sanh.* 3:3, 4, 5; 5:1, 2.

Fourth, the only court empowered to hear a capital case was the court of twenty-three men all ordained in the Land of Israel.[10] Rabbinic tradition acknowledges that this court ceased to exist well before the second Temple was destroyed in 70 C.E.; it also had been required to relocate from the Temple Mount to a place nearby (*b.Sanh.* 41a.) The exact time and circumstances of the demise of the court of twenty-three are a subject of debate among scholars but the court no longer existed by the time the Romans conquered Jerusalem. The competent court under the classic rules simply did not exist long before the tannaitic period came to a close.

Fifth, a conviction under the classic rules required a majority of two votes in the court of twenty-three. An acquittal needed only a majority of one.[11] The court deliberated two consecutive days over a capital case. If a judge had originally argued for acquittal, he was not allowed to change his vote to guilty on the second day, but he could change from guilty to innocent. Actually in a close case a majority of three would have been necessary for conviction: arithmetically 13-10 is the minimum for conviction, while 12-11 suffices for acquittal.

Sixth, the most glaring problem facing the prosecution under the classic rules is the matter of the formal warning, which must be tendered the person who is clearly about to commit the criminal act.[12] That warning must notify the person that what he (or she) is about to do is punishable by a death sentence. The person must acknowledge the warning and explicitly reject it: he or she will persevere in the offense. Without this process of warning and rejection no conviction can occur. The requirement flies in the face of reality. It is simply not reasonable that a person actually about to commit the crime will break off his or her action and respond. The person would either flee the scene — a salutary outcome — or commit the act and then flee.

This process also raises a question about the role the witnesses play. The potential murderer is clearly a *rodef*, a pursuer, whom others may prevent from performing the criminal act, even at the cost of the potential perpetrator's life if no lesser degree of force will stop him (or her). Why then did the witnesses not stop the person?[13] On further reflection, of course, a person, particularly if armed, is not someone the bystander witnesses may care to tackle. The perpetrator who persists will probably have ample opportunity to flee.

As has been already noted, the many capital offenses covered under classic rules are simply not prosecutable (in a human court at least) when committed in darkness or in an out of the way location. Further, the perpetrator may wear

---

10 *m.Sanh.* 1:4 *et passim.*
11 *m.Sanh.* 1:6.
12 *b.Sanh.* 8b, *et passim.*
13 *b.Sanh.*, 73a *mishnah* and *gemara*. See also Stephen M. Passamaneck, "The Jewish Mandate of Martyrdom: Logic and Illogic in the Halakhah," *HUCA* 74 (2003).

a mask, or other disguise, thus seriously impairing the possibility of accurate identification even by upstanding adult male citizens. Even under the classic rules, however, a murderer concerning whom witnesses differed on relatively minor points, but concurred on the major ones, or to whom the warning was not tendered, or whose two witnesses were not in a reasonably close proximity to each other, did not escape entirely. Such a person was taken to the *kippah*, a cell where he was condemned to eat a diet that would cause his intestines to rupture — a sure cause of death in those days.[14] The biblical offenses which were punishable by *karet*, which the Rabbis understood as untimely death at the hands of Heaven, could be erased from the books if the culprit received flagellation (specified in Scripture for certain offenses). Since this flagellation was in place of a "death" penalty some of the same stringencies applied to it, for example, the necessity for a warning. If a culprit had been flogged, twice — for two *karet* criminal acts — and committed a third *karet* act, that person could also be condemned to the *kippah*.[15] There is no mention of anyone who actually received punishment of *kippah,* and given the enormous problems that the prosecution would have had to overcome, it is unlikely that such punishment was ever actually inflicted.

Notwithstanding the clarity of the classic rules, rabbinic tradition does retain instances of capital punishment which occurred before the end of the Second Temple period and clearly in violation of the classic rules. There was the case of Shimon b. Shetah who executed 80 women in one day on charges of witchcraft, a most serious departure from the classic rules that did not allow multiple executions in one day, *b.Sanh.* 45b, 46a. The Talmud takes great pains to justify what he did as an emergency measure which forms no precedent, however, for future situations. There is also the case of the priest's daughter who had been sexually promiscuous, *m.Sanh.* 7:2. A Rabbi recollected that he had seen her executed by burning, although the punishment was not carried out according to the classical rules. The court, so it is stated, was not learned in the rules governing execution by burning, but one finds no exception taken to the fact that she was executed nonetheless.[16]

As a matter of fact, the classic rules were augmented by a rule which allowed an ordinary court to impose punishment, even capital punishment, when in its estimation a situation demanded special measures to protect the community from wrongdoing and Jewish law from ignominy. This is exigency jurisdiction: we shall encounter such special measures in the course of this inquiry.

14 *b.Sanh.* 81b, *mishnah* and *gemara* to the second brief *mishnah.*
15 *b.Sanh.* 81b.
16 The improper procedure had to do with the manner in which the execution was carried out. There is no indication, however, that the sentence of the court or any procedural flaw marred the conviction. No objection is raised to the fact of the execution, only to its manner.

It will become very clear indeed that this exigency procedure, and not the classic rules, was at the heart of medieval Jewish criminal justice.

Before we leave these classic rules, we revert to Enker's and Kirschenbaum's thesis that the criminal code — in its classic form — served primarily religio-educational purposes, which were more important than a societal function of maintaining the public peace and order. Those who properly laud the morality and humanity of the classic rules rarely raise the matter of public safety. This leaves us with a serious ethical question regarding Jewish criminal law: does it protect society? This question was broached albeit obliquely in *m.Mak.* 1:10. There Rabban Simeon b. Gamaliel offers a sharp rejoinder to two of the most illustrious Sages of the late first century C.E., R. Akiba and R. Tarfon. Those two asserted that if they had been on a court of twenty-three, no one ever would have been convicted, to which R. Simeon was moved to declare, "They would have increased the number of murderers at large in Israel." Actually, neither man could have put this boast into effect; by their days the court of twenty-three had long since ceased to exist. Rabban Simeon b. Gamaliel tells us in effect that the classic rules that R. Akiba and R. Tarfon would have applied rigorously would not have served to protect society. R. Akiba and R. Tarfon allowed laudable humanity to work to the detriment of society. Kirschenbaum's balancing of the two purposes of the criminal law — religio-educational as against public safety and public order — leaves us with the conclusion that the classic rules did not protect society, and did not enhance peace and order. They were indeed not intended to do so according to Kirschenbaum; one would imagine that this is hardly a religio-educational goal or ethical ideal that we would want Jewish criminal law to teach. Morality and humanity should also give due regard to the needs and requirements of society as a whole, not just to the fate of the offender. If the classic rules are, as Kirschenbaum characterizes them, "an exercise in exoneration," then a valid corollary comes into focus: these rules disregard public safety and society therefore lies at the mercy of the vicious and violent.[17] One cannot have it both ways: are these rules a matter of exalted morality or a program of criminal justice? They appear as the latter, but emerge as the former!

In the medieval Spanish period of Jewish History, the period that yields much of the material for this study, a leading rabbinic authority also implicitly raised the question of whether or not the classic system really served society. I shall let the authority, R. Solomon b. Adret, the *Rashba*, Spain 1235–1310, speak for himself through his responsum as it appears in *Beth Yosef* to *Tur Hoshen*

---

17 One may suggest that the religio-ethical lessons of the classical rules should be seen as distinct from their (theoretical) purpose of effecting criminal justice. But this really begs the question. They are rules that purport to do both. Yet they cannot effectively do so. Therein lies the conundrum. See Aaron Kirschenbaum, *Introduction to Jewish Law* (Herzliah: Interdisciplinary Center, 2005) 129, 130, for the "exercise in exoneration."

Mishpat 2.[18] There he is commenting on the argumentation for the exigency rules in which the rabbinic court of three may impose severe punishments, notwithstanding the absence of the classic system of criminal justice, when the unfortunate pressures of the time require the Rabbis to curb wanton lawlessness and dissolute behavior. The text is very clear on the matter; Rabbi Solomon b. Adret wrote in a responsum:

> I approve [the view that] if the selectmen believe the witnesses, the selectmen are authorized to impose fines or corporal punishment as it may seem meet to them. This is for the maintenance of the world.[19] If you were to base everything on the laws collected in the Torah, and were only to impose such penalties that Torah provided with respect to cases of wounding, etc., the world would be destroyed, because then we would require the classic procedural elements of the two adult male witnesses and the formal warning. It is as the Sages wrote (*b.B.Meṣ.* 30b) Jerusalem was destroyed because they based their legal rulings only on strict Torah law [that is, the judges did not go beyond the strict limits of Torah law and public order and safety suffered grievously because of that]. How much the more is this true [that judgments may not and must not be founded on the strict limits of Torah law also] outside the land of Israel, where we do not adjudicate matters of fines [certain pecuniary penalties specified in Scripture that also required ordained judges], and consequently reckless persons break through [the protective] barriers of civilized society and the world is devastated [by their depredations].
>
> Our Sages of blessed memory have imposed fines on those who strike another with the hand or knee, as in *b.B.Qam.* 90a even though these penalties, as a matter of pecuniary fines, are not to be adjudicated outside the land of Israel [lit. in Babylonia]. In any event we do occasionally adjudicate [cases of battery] and the like to erect a fence around the generation [to protect them from lawlessness]. Greater [in significance] than this, they said in *b.Sanh.* 45b, 46a that Simeon b. Shetah hanged eighty women in Askelon on one day even though women are not hanged and two capital cases are not heard on one day! It was asserted there that the reason behind Simeon b. Shetah's act was not to transgress the Torah but to build a fence around the Torah. [That reason: the fence around the Torah,] was stated in

18 The *responsum* is identified as *Responsa of R. Solomon b. Adret* attributed to Nahmanides (Solomon b. Adret, *Responsa of R. Solomon b. Adret* [7 vols.; Tel Aviv: Sifriyati, 1957–65] 7:279). See below, chap. 1, n. 1, Hanina Ben Menachem and Neil S. Hecht, *Selected Topics in Jewish Law* (2nd ed.; Boston: Institute of Jewish Law, 1988) 2:44.

19 The Hebrew is *qi'um ha'olam*, a phrase not as well known as *tiqqun ha'olam*. *Tiqqun* emphasizes repair and restoration. *Qi'um* emphasizes maintenance and establishment of a working regime.

b. Yebam. 90b [as a justification with respect to the capital penalty of stoning imposed on the man who rode a horse on the Sabbath and with respect to the flogging penalty imposed on the man who had sex with his wife under a fig tree, that is, in a public place]. All this [matter of special punishment — the witches, the equestrian and the lusty husband] occurred because the circumstances of the time required such procedures.

Sages have followed the very same pattern whenever and wherever they have seen that the circumstances require [the court] to impose punishment on young fools who turn aside to perverse paths. They have said (*b.Sanh.* 58b) that R. Huna in Babylonia had a person's hand amputated [as a punishment for battery]. And in *b.Sanh.* 27a, the Resh Galutha declared that if indeed the accused had killed a person they should blind his eyes. [R. Huna and the Resh Galutha spoke in this manner even though the Rabbis held that mutilation of body parts is not among the punishments specified in the Torah (*b.B.Qam.* 83b, 84a)]. Everything [in these cases] was for the purpose of creating a fence around the Torah and because of the necessity of circumstance.

Therefore if these selectmen have acted and perceived that the circumstance required corporal punishment and a fine for the proper regulation of the region, they have acted lawfully. How much the more is it the proper [course of action] when there is royal license to do so. This is like the case of R. Elazar b. R. Shimon (*b.B.Meṣ.* 83b).

In any event, the selectmen must reflect deeply on the matters and act [only] after consultation. Their intention [in the adjudication of this case] must be solely for the sake of heaven [that is, they must act from the purest motives without any ulterior motive or agenda].

In another responsum, R. Solomon b. Adret wrote that "with respect to capital cases [the judges] must be forewarned to act with the agreement of elders of the city that they act upon the pressing need of time and with deliberation. . . ."

There was indeed a clear concept that public peace and order needed protection. The modalities for that protection form our subject here. To be quite clear: the use of the term modality does not involve technique of formulation or expression. That is, whether a matter is expressed as a single opinion (a responsum) or as a communal ordinance is not here in point. Modality as it is used here means only the specific technique, procedure or penalty that was used to punish, prevent, coerce, or protect as the case may be.

The modalities for the maintenance of public order and public safety fall generally into three areas. First is the area of punitive modalities, which obviously sanctioned punishment of various types, including the capital penalty. There may be punishment for an act committed, which if unpunished and possibly emulated, may undermine public order. The second category involves modalities imposed for the purpose of preventing a wrongful act from occurring, and coercive modalities, which are intended to force an individual to comply with the lawful orders of the rabbinic court or the communal leadership as the case may be. The third category deals with protective modalities which keep persons and property out of harm's way. The various modalities often do appear in the context of responsa which I have condensed here. I have provided information, so far as it is given, on the specific threat or breach affecting public order or safety and the specific modality or modalities, by which a Rabbi or community proposed to deal with the threat or breach. No attempt is made here to categorize all modalities or all situations with respect to maintenance of public order and safety. It is hoped, however, that the material presented is sufficiently illustrative and representative.

Punitive Modalities

This first category includes the most serious modalities, up to and including capital punishment. Capital punishment in medieval Jewish law requires a closer look at a rule of exigency jurisdiction which appears in the Babylonian Talmud. The principle of exigency jurisdiction appears twice, *b.Yebam.* 90b and *b.Sanh.* 46a.[1] The *Yebamot* passage is the more instructive because it appears at the end of a series of amoraic exchanges which explore the power and the authority of the rabbinic court. The text is foundational for the development of Jewish criminal law in the Middle Ages, particularly in various Spanish communities, and it speaks directly to the matter of good public order.

The two cases examining the authority of the rabbinic court that immediately precede the key text in *Yebamot* set the stage, clearly enunciating the enormous reach of rabbinic power, when Rabbis actually wielded such power. The *gemara* cites Deut 18:15 on the matter of prophetic authority: "A prophet will the Lord thy God raise up . . . unto him you will listen." The anonymous commentator of the *gemara* gives wide scope to this the biblical requirement: even if he tells you to transgress a biblical commandment, you are to listen to him. The case of Elijah at Mount Carmel is then added to illustrate this situation (1 Kgs 18:25–38). Elijah offered unlawful sacrifice in order to keep the people from the gross transgressions of idolatry. This was an emergency measure specifically for that occasion. The *gemara* explains that Elijah's case differed from a rabbinic ordinance because the orders of a true prophet, like Elijah, are covered by Deut 18:15: of course one must listen to a prophet. An anonymous voice then suggests that the authority of the court to institute a special measure in a particular emergency could be derived from Elijah's experience. This suggestion is rejected: a special punitive measure is a different matter. Presumably what Elijah did was, as the rabbis viewed it, covered by the Deuteronomy passage and it formed no precedent. Further, as we shall see, a special punitive measure does not contravene biblical law, it surrounds it with an additional layer of regulation.

The next element of this discussion in *Bavli Yebamot* then takes up the matter of the instrument of divorce. R. Simeon ben Gamaliel does not permit a man to nullify such an instrument, which he had duly authorized a rabbinic court to prepare for his wife, nor may the man add stipulations to it. The wife in this situation is presumed to be unaware of the divorce proceedings; the instrument which was entrusted to an agent for delivery has not yet reached her hand. Implicit in this rule is that the man, not the court, has the legal authority

---

1 On the subject of exigency jurisdiction see Ben Menachem and Hecht, *Selected Topics in Jewish Law*, vol. 2. This book gives a most thorough review of the jurisprudence intricacies of the matter.

under biblical law to authorize the instrument of divorce. R. Simeon ben
Gamaliel reasons that if the man could nullify (or alter) the instrument by con-
vening another court for that purpose, the woman, under the impression that
the original instrument was valid, might remarry, even though she was still her
first husband's lawful wife. What actual power then could the court be said to
possess? The court had already become an accessory to the husband's absolute
power of divorce. The ordinance was instituted as a matter of good public policy.

The *gemara* considers this situation and asks if the principle of the power
of the rabbinic court is indeed sufficient to override the fact that under biblical
law the instrument was nullified. The answer is affirmative. The rabbis assert the
principle that any man who marries implicitly accepts the rabbinic rules and
regulations for the marriage regimen in their entirety: the rabbis have authority over every marriage and may nullify the marriage.[2] It becomes as though it
had never occurred. The rabbis then discuss the implications of this principle
with respect to marriage affected by money payment or by sexual intercourse.

The idea of a special measure is implicit here. The rabbis assert superinten-
dence over marriages which every bridegroom implicitly accepts through the
very process of marrying. The rabbis have in effect declared that their rules and
regulations form, so to speak, an outer layer of protection around the biblical
rules of marriage (and divorce). The court sees to the enforcement of this protective barrier against abuse such as the nullification of a divorce about which
the hapless wife knows nothing.

The *gemara* now states the text which explicitly establishes the court's exigency jurisdiction in other situations. R. Eliezer b. Ya'akov states that he has
heard that the rabbinic court imposed floggings and punishment not provided
under Torah law. This step did not transgress Torah law but erected a protective barrier around it. The case involved an incident of a man who rode a horse
on the Sabbath. This event is placed in the Greek period. They brought him to
the court and executed him by stoning, not because this was his proper punishment (riding a horse per se is not a violation of the Sabbath) but because "the
times" warranted such a severe measure. And there was another incident of a
man who had sexual intercourse with his wife under a fig tree (that is, where
they could be seen) and they brought him to court and flogged him, not because this was the proper punishment but because "the times" warranted such
a severe measure. The *gemara* quickly adds that special measures in the law are
"different." This last statement implies such severe measures are not precedents
for future incidents. Each exercise of this special power is thus considered a
fresh situation, to be handled on its own merits. What is clear and indeed very

2 *Kol d'miqadesh a'da'ata d'rabbanan miqadesh,* see also *b.Ketub.* 3a, *et passim.*

clear is that the exigency jurisdiction, the power and authority to take special measures as a "fence for the law," belonged to the rabbinic court. They exercised it as they believed the situation required them to exercise it. They enforced the law just as Elijah had broken it: to protect it from greater harm.

When did this power become part of the rabbinic legal arsenal? That cannot be established with any accuracy. R. Eliezer b. Ya'akov was a first-century C.E. figure, known for the high quality of his rulings. The reference to the quote "Greek period" is understood by Rashi to mean troublous times when the Jews transgressed the law rather freely. The "Greek period" also suggests a time well before the destruction of the Second Temple in 70 C.E. This enormous power to impose extraordinary punishment appears to go back to a period when presumably the classic rules, or some form of them, were operative. This jurisdiction does not seem to be some late invention. It is an effective and practical principle for maintaining public safety and public order, the constant task of criminal justice, perhaps because the classical rules did not really suffice for the purpose. The use of this power was available whenever the situation demanded serious intervention to forestall unacceptable types of behavior.

The second appearance of the R. Eliezer b. Ya'akov text occurs in *b.Sanh.* 46a. The wording is exactly the same. It comes as a postscript to the report that Simeon b. Shetah hanged eighty women on one day, even though under classic procedure two culprits are not to be tried on the same day. The *gemara* is at great pains to demonstrate that multiple cases of the same offense, each carrying the same form of execution, may be tried on the same day. Yet in Simeon b. Shetah's situation, the women were involved with two different forms of witchcraft and thus were not all tried for the same offense. Thus Simeon b. Shetah relied on the emergency power of the court, which the Eliezer b. Ya'akov text describes. Here indeed the emergency power is invoked to override the law against multiple executions. In this case, he "breaks" the law to preserve it from greater harms just as Elijah had done at Mount Carmel.

The *gemara*'s implications that Simeon b. Shetah invoked emergency authority again suggest that such authority had become part of the powers of the rabbinic court rather early on. The *gemara* does not provide abundant detail about trial of the eighty women. In Simeon b. Shetah's era the classic rules (or some form of them) presumably were operative since this same figure, when coming upon a man with a bloody knife standing over a dying man, declared that no trial could proceed because there had not been the requisite number of witnesses. In that case, however, exigency power of the court became unnecessary when a venomous snake bit the murderer and he forthwith died (*b.Sanh.* 37b). Tradition holds that divine justice had taken care of the matter. In any event, we do not know how the eighty witches were tried: what sort of court, working under what sort of rules. Some aspect of exigency jurisdiction is at least possible in the case, though the actual details of the matter are long lost in the shadows of history.

The principle of exigency jurisdiction is clearly established in rabbinic law through the anecdote concerning R. Eliezer b. Zadok, and it is arguably a rather early feature of it. Further, the rabbis were the authorities who had the power to "declare" an emergency, that is, what was, and what was not, such a situation. They also had the authority to adapt and adopt whatever rules of evidence and procedure they believed to be suitable for cases involving emergency measures for the general welfare of the community, its public peace and order.

We shall now look at cases that show us just how the rabbinic justice system actually functioned. These are the medieval cases. The ancient text that explicitly describes emergency jurisdiction gave examples in which procedures were undertaken in order to suppress behavior that was suggestive of transgression; but while it was not actually unlawful, it was still an affront to public morals and religious sensitivity. The medieval cases for their part do deal with serious "criminal" breeches of the peace.

Two Cases of Homicide

We first look at two cases of homicide, clearly a most serious breech of public order and safety. One of them was apparently premeditated; the other may have been a spur of the moment event. They are both treated as willful killings.

The cases come from the responsa of R. Judah b. Asher collected in the volume *Zichron Yehudah*.[3] Judah b. Asher, son of the great R. Asher b. Yehiel, the *Rosh*, succeeded his father as the major Jewish legal authority of Toledo after the *Rosh*'s death in 1327. He was also the brother of R. Jacob b. Asher, *Ba'al ha-Turim*. The cases are therefore from the mid-fourteenth century.

CASE ONE

The text of responsum 79 launches into a rehearsal of events in Cordova without any preliminary salutations. It seems that a judge, one of the honored men of the city, ruled that a certain Jew had to pay a certain sum he owed in taxes and he ordered that the man be seized for this. In the dark of the night, when the judge was walking to the synagogue, the delinquent taxpayer, apparently lurking in the shadows, leaped out and stabbed the judge twice, inflicting mortal wounds. No witness saw the attack, but the suspect had made threats prior to the attack. People did see him lurking about in apparent ambush prior to the at-

3 Judah b. Asher, *Responsa Zichron Yehudah* (Berlin: Friedlander, 1846. Repr.; Jerusalem, 1967). See also Stephen M. Passameneck, "R. Judah b. Asher on Capital Punishment," *Jewish Law Association Studies* 7 (1994) 153–72.

tack. The suspect then fled. At this point the responsum asserts that an excommunicatory ban was pronounced against him: he should come forward to pay the tax judgment against him on pain of excommunication for non-compliance. He did not come forward.

The assassination of a judge by a disaffected taxpayer is nothing to be taken lightly – a serious breach of the peace indeed.

R. Judah proceeds with his response. He addresses it to the sages and honorable gentlemen of the community of Cordova. He gives the name of the judge and his presumed assailant. He remarks that there are qualified sages in Seville, a city closer to Cordova than Toledo. After the appropriate disclaimers that he is not really worthy to be called upon for an answer when there are so many other eminently qualified persons the questioners could ask, he does deliver his detailed, and impassioned, answer as to what should be done in this case which has all of the appearances of a premeditated homicide, where the victim is a figure of some note and in fact a part of the justice system.

He writes, "First of all I say that it is most necessary for every court which seeks justice to maintain and augment the protective measures instituted by our sages as the times may require. They are protective measures for the essential elements of Torah." He reasons that talmudic sages instituted secondary degrees of forbidden marital unions as a means of keeping the biblical degrees of forbidden unions inviolate;[4] they instituted regulations on the cleanliness of hands to protect the cleanliness of *terumah*, and also developed rules on Sabbath limits, rabbinically extending ordinances regarding Sabbath rest so that the biblical laws of Sabbath rest would not be infringed. R. Judah notes that they were particularly strict in the matter of preventive measures, even going so far as to require the death of a lovelorn young man, by refusing to allow any contact whatsoever between him and the lady with whom he was infatuated, even though such contact would not necessarily have violated any biblical law since the woman was not married.[5]

R. Judah then cites a part of the foundational text of exigency jurisdiction.[6] He notes the incident in which the Sabbath equestrian was stoned to death by the court. He comments that the severe action was taken because the times were rife with apostasy; commandments were treated lightly. In order to wall off the breach which had occurred in proper Jewish life and observance, the court took extreme measures. Obviously such a breach of religious practice and the observance of religious commandments amounts to a breach of public order – and public safety – for the Rabbis.

The author's next point is central to the exercise of exigency jurisdiction. He

4 See *b. Yebam.* 21b, and *Mishnah Yadayim* goes into the matters on cleanliness at great length.
5 *b.Sanh.* 75a.
6 The reminiscence of R. Eliezer b. Zadok which we have already examined.

asserts widespread acknowledgement that fresh events are innumerable and it is impossible before the fact to take account of them and define all the legal rules pertaining to them. Therefore the Sages wrote a general principle (for our guidance) under which many matters are subsumed. They granted the court the authority and power to take special measures, at all times, as the times might require. R. Judah then cites the text of *b.Sanh.* 46a in full, the special measures taken when the times demanded swift and severe action. The court is clothed with an inherent power to do what is necessary to preserve public order and public safety.

R. Judah returns to the specific question at hand. He writes that the law is an indispensable pillar of civilized society; and were it not for the judge, any person more powerful than another could simply swallow him up. The judges established the laws on their foundations; they are compared to kings, *b.Ketub.* 105b, and tradition cautions us to honor judges — how much the more are we not to despise them — even when a judge is not sitting on a case! And how much the more is the person of a judge to be treated with respect when he has made a properly founded ruling — and even more, he is not to be injured!

He further says that in this case even if the victim had not been a judge, and the assailant had lain in wait and struck a cruel blow, it would have been proper to amputate the culprit's hand, that the arm of the wicked be broken (Ps 10:15). He then rises to a new level: if a person had injured a court officer, who was acting under the authority of the court, it would have been proper to punish him even more severely — how much the more that the victim was indeed the judge himself, who had given a correct judgment!

As far as Judah b. Asher is concerned, the case is a clear cut matter of the premeditated assassination of a judge. The peace and good order of society have been brutally assaulted through this vicious act. This situation demands action, and the action is sanctioned by exigency jurisdiction. The question now is, on the basis of the case that can be made against the suspect who has fled, what should be done once he should be caught — if he ever is.

R. Judah marshals the "evidence" against the suspect. No witnesses saw the actual attack, but there is a presumption based on a persistent rumor in the city that the suspect is guilty. He mentions "plausible reasons" to assert his guilt and mentions the witnesses who saw him loitering in ambush with his cloak over his eyes — in order to prevent recognition! After the event, the suspect fled and has not been seen in town since even though excommunication was pronounced against him to come forward to satisfy the judgment against him. R. Judah simply declares that everyone considers him the culprit as if they had seem him strike the mortal blows with their own eyes.

This is not anywhere near the sort of "evidence" that would pass muster under the classic rules. It is hardly "evidence" at all. The only real statement against him is the matter of his loitering in ambush — with his face hooded. But even that occurred at night. The sighting, even if accurate, only puts him at or near the location of the attack. It does not prove he did it. The fact that he fled could be explained: after the event he knew that he would be the prime suspect so he ran away to protect himself. Everything else is presumption and rumor. Yet all this is modern speculation long after the fact. In the event, his guilt was taken as proven.

Moreover, it becomes perfectly clear that the Rabbi wished to make an example of him. His fate was to become an example to the people that such an act could not and would not be tolerated. He says that it appears proper to him to impose punishment as if there had been witnesses to the act since the punishment is for the purpose of preventing any reoccurrence of such a deed. Every judge should be able to administer justice without fear of harm from unsuccessful litigants.

R. Judah has already gone on record as supporting amputation as the punishment he suggests: "The arm of the wicked should be broken." This penalty will be a visible lesson to others not to commit such outrages, and it will eliminate the capacity of this particular offender to do so. Punishment is exemplary, and deterrent — with respect to the offender.

He then goes on to draw distinction between this premeditated homicide against a judge, which if not suitably punished, could invite other disaffected persons to follow suit, and homicides committed in the heat of passion, during a quarrel, where there is really no need to institute any special measures. In the crimes of passion the offender is to be convicted on the testimony of witnesses, and then duly punished. But in an emergency when a special measure is necessary, upon "verification of the facts" (by whatever means, even when they are rather suspect) the court imposes punishment. Punishment must be meted out by such means as the court shall think proper as long as the court is acting with the intent of achieving true justice — and has no unworthy and additional agenda. The very nature of the case established for R. Judah a special circumstance, and the witnesses who would be required, if capital punishment were to be an option, are not apparently necessary here when some lesser penalty may be prescribed. The penalty of amputation of the hand will fully serve the purposes of exemplary and exigent justice. The assassination of a judge is of course an exigent matter — but not in this instance a capital one since no actual witnesses exist.

R. Judah concludes by clearly stating that in this situation he would not recommend the capital penalty though by no means is such a penalty excluded from the modalities available to maintain public order. The amputation will serve as a constant reminder of the offender's act. To quote Ps 59:12, "Slay them not, lest people forget." In his final paragraph he reports that he debated this matter with the scholars and sages of Toledo, and a majority, with whom he agrees, decided that should a similar case arise in their community, they would amputate *both* the offender's hands because he struck *two* blows.

The Cordovan outrage presents a clear and compelling instance of a breach of the peace and a threat to public order. It required a special emergency remedy. The rabbis suggest two modalities in the course of his decision. Capital punishment is not endorsed only because the so-called "evidence" is wholly insufficient. Amputation of one (or both?) hands is the recommended penalty even though the "evidence" is not much more than a suspicious sighting of the offender and rumor. No matter: judges must not be afraid to render true judgments. One finds no record of the final disposition of the case: was he ever caught and punished?

CASE TWO

The second case, also from the pen of R. Judah b. Asher, also requires an emergency measure; the classic rules are never of course invoked in this case of homicide, but capital punishment is. In this case however, one finds more evidence against the offender. The case is responsum 58 of *Zichron Yehudah,* and the homicide occurred once again in Cordova.

After a flowery introduction and greeting to his inquirers, R. Judah says that the letter that reached him concerned the blows which Saul gave Isaac, and the testimonies on the matter, and also complaints that Saul raised against the testimony. The author relates that the inquirers wish to take counsel with him. They want him to write what seemed to be the proper punishment for the accused Saul, and whether or not they should explore the veracity of the points Saul raised concerning the testimony against him and, if true, is that testimony thereby nullified.

R. Judah commences his response proper by reminding the inquirers that the classic forms of capital punishment have not been in force since the Sanhedrin ceased to sit in the Hall of Hewn Stone, and whatever form the law may take now is for the purpose of erecting a preventive rule to stem the wantonness of the generation.

He offers a paean to the king's wisdom, "Praise God who has inclined the heart of the King of this land to give the Jews the power to judge and remove evildoers among them." Were it not for this [royal privilege] the Jews could not survive in the country. Moreover, how many Jews are saved by Jewish judges [that is, when they are tried under Jewish law] who would be put to death by non-Jewish judges, presumably for the same crime. The author then states in summation of this portion of the responsum that the laws the Jews use in capital cases are not all according to Torah law. This sentence makes two important points that he wants his correspondents to understand: first, Jews do employ the punitive modality of capital punishment and second, the procedures under which it is decreed do not accord with the classic Torah rules. The correspondents doubtless already knew that but R. Judah puts it clearly on the record.

R. Judah says he will write what he perceives to be the correct procedures on the basis of what he has observed in his home city.

First of all, he writes, it is necessary to ascertain the veracity of Saul's claims about the testimony against him. He presents the proper procedure for doing this. The court of record is not, however, to issue a call, under penalty of excommunication for non-compliance, for people to come forward and testify should they have information that any of the witnesses is suspected of having violated the law. This procedure is a *pesquisa* and it is unlawful.[7] If, however, people come forward of their own accord to discredit any of the witnesses, one may issue an excommunicatory ban in their presence in order to impress them to tell the truth. If it should appear that one of the witnesses against Saul has transgressed a biblical negative commandment, that person's testimony will not be recognized. If the person has become unfit to testify because of a transgression of a rabbinical ordinance, the testimony he has already given is still acceptable.

The author proceeds to inform the inquirers that nowadays it is customary to accept the testimony of persons as long as no evidence exists that such a person is manifestly halakhically unfit to testify. In this matter, he writes, we rely on the statement in *b.Ḥag.* 22a that testimony may be accepted from *amé ha'aretz,* that is, from persons whose regimen of piety may not be perfect, but who are certainly not lawbreakers. The talmudic opinion is in the name of R. Jose. Thus, he concludes, you will be able to tell which testimony is acceptable and which is not. That determination ultimately, of course, rests with the inquirers.

He moves on. They asked him for his opinion on the fact that the accused transgressed grievously – to deliver such a brutal blow – because it is from simple, ordinary people that this matter has become public knowledge: that he struck the deceased a mortal blow; and that he admitted to the act and that his flight is testimony against him, and that he paid medical expenses for the victim. Briefly put, they asked him what he would do on the basis of the evidence they sent to him. He clarifies the nature of the testimony and then proceeds to offer reasoned advice.

Moses Pishlish (?) and Abraham Halud testified that they saw him (Saul)

---

7 *Pesquisa* is a term for judicial, inquisitional, investigation. See Stephen M. Passamaneck, "Remarks on Pesquisa in Medieval Jewish Legal Procedure," *Jewish Law Association Studies* 9 (1996).

deliver the mortal blow to the deceased. Joseph b. Avid and Isaac b. Yom Tov depose that they saw the two (Saul and Isaac) quarreling. They left the scene and when they returned they saw Isaac on the ground with a bleeding head wound. Other testimony sent to R. Judah is not, in his opinion, of any value in the matter. Joseph Avid and Isaac b. Yom Tov are cousins and are considered as one single witness owing to their family relationship. Other testimony is not compromised in this fashion. R. Judah asserts that the rule that if a pair of witnesses is found to be related to each other or one is found unfit to testify (for example, he is a professional gambler) both members of the pair are disqualified only applies when people have stepped forward of their own accord to testify. When, however, they appear because of the coercive power of a ban (a *pesquisa*?) and they are thus compelled to come forward, the testimony of the two of them is not wholly invalidated if they are found to be relatives or one is found to be disqualified from testifying. R. Judah cites this last rule as the opinion of his father.

At length R. Judah comes to the matter of punishment that he recommends in this case of homicide. The matter here is serious, of course, but it is not the public outrage of the assassination case. Here we have a homicide presumably on the spur of the moment in the course of a violent quarrel. Even though the offender Saul apparently shows some remorse — how else to explain his contribution to medical costs — he is nonetheless a murderer. R. Judah reviews five possible modalities for the restoration of peace and order in this matter of homicide committed by Saul. He notes that these modalities are the usual and customary penalties in capital cases.

First, if the testimony of both Moses and Abraham is believed, he is to be put to death. Second, if the testimony of only one of those two is believed, along with the testimony of either Joseph or Isaac, he should have both hands amputated. Third, if the testimony of either Moses or Abraham is sustained but the testimony of both Joseph and Isaac is not, he is to have his right hand amputated. Fourth, if the testimony of Moses and Abraham is not sustained, but the testimony of Joseph (or) Isaac is sustained, he is to have his left hand amputated, on the basis of the testimony of one of them taken conjointly with the well known public perception that he committed the homicide. Fifth, if none of the testimony is sustained then he is to be condemned to exile from the community because of the public perception that he killed the man; the author describes this as fulfillment of the biblical verse "You shall remove the evil from your midst" (Deut 13:6 *et passim*).

In this case, apparently sufficient evidence existed for justice to take its course under the royal privilege of capital jurisdiction enjoyed by the Jews of Cordova. R. Judah b. Asher is not at all reticent in his praise for this privilege. It is a key element for him in the maintenance of Jewish life in the country, which clearly equates to the maintenance of public order and public safety by any reasonable standard. Without a moment's hesitation he lists the punitive modalities for homicide (even without invoking exigency power, presumably royal warrant alone is sufficient!) – death, various mutilations, and finally exile. One finds no record as to the ultimate apprehension and punishment of the offender Saul.

Two Other Great Rabbinic Masters

The remarks of two other of the great rabbinic masters who dealt with the punitive measures expand upon their importance, their scope, and finally the procedures used in such cases.

R. Yom Tov b. Abraham Ashbili, d. 1330, memorialized the king himself on the particulars of a case involving the penalty of amputation that came to royal notice. R. Yom Tov is known by the acronym *Ritba*.[8]

A man by the name of Saul had suffered amputation of the hand as punishment, apparently for homicide. This is most probably not the same Saul we met in R. Judah b. Asher's case; too many details do not match up, and the facts examined by R. Judah are not reviewed in this case. In the absence of sufficient detail it is best not to see them as the same matter. More than one Saul could have been an offender. This Saul took exception to the way his trial had been conducted and raised eight complaints against the trial judge and the testimony against him. The judge answered each of the eight points to R. Yom Tov's satisfaction and then he added his own commentary to the judge's response, finally addressing the king directly. The king had indeed turned to *Ritba* as his consultant on Jewish matters, particularly matters of Jewish law.

First *Ritba* exonerates the judge from any blame with respect to the penalty of amputation of the hand and other matters, because he relied in this matter on the advice of a gentleman in the district who is a scholar and upon whom judges rely for advice in their conduct of trials.

The *Ritba* explains matters of "special measures" jurisprudence to the king in detail. The points that Saul had raised apply to the settlement of quarrels between individuals. In matters where the judge acts to impose exemplary punishment because of many complaints against the accused in order to maintain public safety and order, to expunge wickedness and to erect the protective barrier around the Torah, none of Saul's points is relevant. The law is not merely for the particular injured parties, it is just as much for the rest of society: that wrongdoers not become accustomed to act wrongfully and the rest of the people will hear of and observe their anti-social activity. Even if his victims forgave him for what he did to them, which they apparently did according to Saul's statement, yet he persists in his wickedness; how much the more, declares *Ritba*, does he deserve exemplary punishment.

8 Joseph Kafah, *Responsa of Yom Tov b. Abraham Ashbili* (Jerusalem: Mossad Harav Kuk, 1958) no. 131.

Ritba then makes his most telling point. The judge may try such a repeat offender even without a complainant. The judge is the "father of the community" and is duty bound to maintain its peace and good order through his legal decisions, as he is duty bound to see to the maintenance of public roadways so that the public does not suffer any injury. The judge is thus, according to *Ritba* in his address to the sovereign, fully empowered to take such measures as may be necessary to curb egregious wrongdoing. The judge's latitude in these matters is enormous. The Rabbi goes even further: since it came out in the testimony against Saul that he had been an informer to gentile authority[9] against Jews, it is the widespread law that such persons are put to death. They are troublers of the community. It further came out that Saul had been involved in bribery, perjury and battery. *Ritba* argues that the judge who is empowered to impose a capital penalty on an informer (see below, p. 35) certainly acts within the law to order amputation of the hand in this matter.

Saul further complained that some of the testimony against him came from persons related to each other, which testimony is ordinarily inadmissible. A local ordinance of the community, adopted by the entire community, provided that the *adelantados* may lawfully use such testimony in the conduct of their public business. Since this case involves the complaint of the public, and was handled as a measure of exemplary punishment, if one were to reject the testimony of "interested parties" the community could never impose such punishment since the community as a whole is an interested party! Thus communities customarily tried such cases with witnesses from the affected community and occasionally with testimony from persons related to each other. He further states that exemplary punishment may be inflicted without any warning when we deal with a repeat offender who is poised to reoffend. He would not heed the warning anyway.

The *Ritba* concludes this portion of his memorial to the king by reiterating that the judge in the case bears no guilt nor cause for punishment for what he did, as long as he imposed exemplary punishment out of fear of Heaven, concern for the public welfare and as a protective barrier for the Torah.

At this point in *Ritba*'s memorial the tone and spirit change from forthright defense of what was done to the miscreant Saul to a merciful consideration of Saul's future. The judge exceeded his adviser's advice in one particular: he exiled the man from his home and his kin in addition to the amputation. This is seen as a bad additional penalty. *Ritba* points out that he is now a handless cripple and can no longer earn a living at his trade. It is therefore proper to rescind

---

9   No more serious and tragic offense appears in the catalogue of medieval Jewish criminal activity. Informing against Jewish persons or property was taken as a matter that could place more than the victim at risk, and thus in a sense it is akin to the modern notion of "crime." Every authority on medieval Jewish life whom I have encountered emphasizes the gravity of the act; it could not be tolerated.

the exile and for the community to provide some means of livelihood for him since he has accepted their rulings. The man whom the community reviled and saw grievously punished for his misdeeds should now receive some rehabilitation from that community. They should find work for him; he should be able to support himself and his family.

The same judge that did not hesitate to concur in the punishment of amputation, and even to suggest that a capital penalty might not have been out of the question, now urges the community to ensure that the man has some sort of useful future. He does this for the man's sake of course, but also for the enlightenment of the community. The man should live in a "bad place," and be a visible object lesson to others. He should be warned to have no dealings with unsavory characters who might be suspect of informing. The warning should also make it clear that any further offense will bring further punishment. He should go about his business with humility. The key to the matter here is that he has accepted his punishment and remains a member of the community. He is still a Jew deserving of whatever kindness and consideration his present circumstances may allow.

This merciful postscript to the memorial does not mitigate the severity of punishments inflicted as special punitive measures. What it does show is simply that the Rabbis could take a larger view of the matter. Indeed they had to punish, and punish they did, but they did not have to leave the crippled wrongdoer to the vagaries of an unknown future. The person was after all a person, and had to function in society both as a breadwinner and an object lesson.

The idea of special punitive jurisprudence with its emphasis on a complaint from the community comes quite close to a modern concept of criminal law and crime: offenses against the peace of the state. In any event, the Jewish communities that wielded the power to take special measures understood well that public safety and public order are essential bases for community life.

The other great Spanish master, Rabbi Isaac B. Sheshet Prefet, the *Rivash* (d. 1408), remarks on this area of jurisprudence in one responsum and in another series of responsa provides an insight into the procedures followed in such cases.[10] *Rivash* explores the matter of the punitive special measure. He begins by underscoring the fact that capital cases, where they are heard at all, are not conducted under the classic rules of the Talmud but through special royal permission to do so. He also summarizes the talmudic bases for invoking the special measure. He cites *b. Yebam.* 90b, the recollection of R. Eliezer b. Ya'akov. He also cites *b. B. Meṣ.* 83b, which relates that R. Elazar b. Shimon, acting under royal commission as both a peace officer and a judge, had Jewish law breakers sentenced to death under his license as judge. This did not endear him to his

---

10 Isaac b. Sheset Prefet, *Responsa of R. Isaac b. Sheshet Prefet* (ed. Constantinople, 1546) no. 251.

colleagues or his co-religionists, but *Rivash* does not mention that.

Rivash also reviews talmudic records of special punishments short of capital sentence. He cites *b.Sanh.* 27b and the incident in which the *Resh Galutha* approved the punishment of blinding if the accused was indeed guilty of murder. He also mentions the case of R. Huna who ordered the amputation of the hand of a man who was a persistent batterer of others (*b.Sanh.* 58b). He notes, however, that in cases decided according to the needs of the hour it is correct to punish the murderer more severely than the batterer and wounder. Similarly, the degree of punishment should properly take into account the amount and quality of evidence against the accused: the certainty of the testimony and circumstantial evidence.

Rivash then takes a close look at the specific case he has been asked to review. It seems that two men killed a third man. He examines a number of arguments against their guilt and rejects them all. Finally he seizes upon one argument that might save the two accused men which he does appear to approve: There were two assailants and one cannot tell which of the two delivered the fatal blow, unless the first rendered the victim *terefah,* so that the second assailant becomes exempt from punishment.[11] It is thus possible to hold the two guiltless in the matter: the true identity of the actual killer can not be established.

He then turns to the matter of the punitive measure. Under this procedure the two assailants, who did in fact kill the deceased, may be put to death. They acted high-handedly and wantonly. They stalked him day and night, in public, in the view of the leadership of the community. The community has the authority to put the two to death if they choose to do so, after the manner of R. Elazar b. Simon who also acted under governmental authority when he imposed capital penalties.

Rivash then suggests another possibility for punishment on the basis of the need of the hour and the need for a special measure. The amputation of the hand may be imposed rather than the death penalty. He adds a personal note: if he were in the place of the judges, acting under royal authority, he would order no lighter penalty than amputation of the hand without the consent of the relatives of the deceased, a novel idea indeed. It is quite sufficient to act leniently to the extent of R. Huna's penalty for those who strike their fellows with a deadly weapon.

Rivash adds a caution. If the deceased had acted in such a manner as to interfere with his recovery from the wounds and according to the physicians he had endangered his own health, and therefore was, as it were, complicit in his own death, one may be more lenient with the assailants. They need not lose a limb,

11 See *b.Sanh.* 78a.

but should be fined, flogged, excommunicated, exiled from the community for a while.

Finally *Rivash* brings new details to light that expose a scandalous situation in that community. Apparently the local judge instigated a homicide. This was an insupportable act of arrogant viciousness carried on in public by a public official! The judge's son also should receive a most stern admonition. He ran after the deceased with a sword in the presence of the communal leadership and received no remonstrance for that behavior. *Rivash* cites the *Mishneh Torah* of Maimonidies, *Hilkhot Rozeah* 2:2, to the effect that one who solicits the murder of another is not himself subject to a death penalty of the human court but is liable under divine law. Nevertheless, *Rivash* opened with the matter of the emergency, the necessity of the hour, so that if a court saw fit to impose punishment on such a person, it has the authority to do so under royal patent.

Rivash has in effect returned to the point he made at the outset. Emergency measures are in order to preserve the public peace and the public safety. The classic rules are insufficient to maintain order in the real world of the Spanish communities if severe punishment is deemed necessary. To pursue public welfare, the judge (the judge in this matter surely excepted!) is the father of the community as *Ritba* wrote, and will act for the sake of Heaven and for the preservation of the public peace.

The texts considered so far have provided some information on the procedures followed in the case of punitive measures. Several further responsa from *Rivash* will round out at least in theory the details of such trials. The subject under notice in those responsa is "informing," which we shall examine in a later section. Informing against Jews or Jewish property to the non-Jewish authorities was treated as one of the most dangerous threats to public welfare and was punishable capitally, an occasion for a special punitive measure. Therefore the procedures surrounding its adjudication as a capital offense appear here with the offense of homicide. The procedures are quite the same.

According to *Rivash*'s responsum 234 in the Constantinople edition, a certain person acted riotously and uttered defamatory statements that brought him up on the charge of informing. *Rivash* dismisses the charges almost immediately, but on the hypothesis that the accused could be guilty, he writes an extremely thorough review of the entire matter (responsa 234 through 239), and in this discussion he illuminates important procedural details. The first of these, covered in no. 234 concerns the confession of the defendant. The inquirers are the *adelantados* of Teruel who do not want to do anything that might be viewed as inquisitorial; inquisitorial procedure is basically a procedure without a complaint in which the judges or their agents "inquire" into the matter themselves. The Spanish is *pesquisa*, a judicial inquisition, a term we have already encountered.[12] Thus arises the matter of the confession: is taking the accused's confession as a first step an (improper!) inquisitorial procedure or should witnesses be heard first?

Rivash commences his discussion with a review of the procedure in pecuniary cases. There witnesses are not heard until after the defendant has answered the charges. The defendant may admit the claims against him, that is, confess to them, and his confession is as good as "one hundred witnesses." Witnesses are heard only after a claim is denied. He also notes the special circumstances in which testimony of witnesses is not taken in the defendant's presence.

He moves on to the "classic rules" of procedure in capital cases. There, a confession, no matter how voluntary or how sincere, is simply not heard. A confession in a capital case has no legal significance under the classic rules.

Under the royal patent, which permits Jewish courts to adjudicate capital cases, matters are very different. *Rivash* points out that it is necessary to prove and substantiate the rulings of the Jewish court to the satisfaction of non-Jewish magistrates, lest the Jews be suspected of improper judgments. Further, classic rules no longer apply since Jewish courts impose capital or corporal punishment as may be required even where no absolute and unimpeachable testimony exists, relying rather upon strong plausible circumstantial evidence of guilt.

Therefore, says *Rivash*, the practice of taking the defendant's confession, if any, in a capital case has developed. This confession, along with other evidentiary statements, there being no unequivocal testimony, has become a tool which the judges use in examination of witnesses. *Rivash* concludes that in this state of affairs, the confession (or statement) of the defendant should be taken before witnesses are heard, yet if the witnesses are heard first, there is no procedural flaw in the prosecution and the confession may be heard after the witnesses have spoken.

The responsum concludes with *Rivash*'s opinion that as long as there is a plaintiff, in some sense, in the case, no real danger of running afoul of the prohibition against inquisitorial procedure current in the kingdom of Aragon exists. According to *Rivash*, he has often witnessed the principal Jewish leaders of a community, sitting as judges, take a confession when there is a complaint. But he says the non-Jewish law is not his area of expertise. In case of questions and doubts in these matters, the community should certainly consult non-Jewish legal authority.

Briefly put: the defendant's confession, anathema under the classic rules, is quite acceptable, even necessary perhaps, in cases of punitive measures involving capital or corporal punishment. The law has turned 180 degrees. None of this, however, should be taken to suggest that a confession would be accept-

12 See above, n. 7.

able if it were coerced. The matter of coercive modalities will be treated below, but no reason at all exists to believe that the confessions contemplated here are anything but honest and quite voluntary. The idea of confession, voluntary and sincere, is moreover important from another point of view. Such an utterance helps to purge an individual of the sinful aspect of his act and may very well help to mitigate the sentence of the court. Confession and remorse carried significant weight in rabbinical circles.

In responsum 235, *Rivash* decides that the defendant in the case, the accused informer, should have an advocate to plead on his behalf in court, especially since the plaintiff has one. His final point in the responsum, however, presents a quite uncharitable view of the advocate. Since the court customarily takes the confession of the accused (there being no reason to believe it is involuntary or coerced), if that confession is taken prior to the appointment of the advocate, no harm is done. The Rabbi is concerned that the advocate might coach him in prevarication and that justice might not therefore be best served; therefore the later appointment is perfectly acceptable practice according to *Rivash*.

In responsum 236 *Rivash* denies bail for this defendant who may be facing a capital charge. Apparently the person had been incarcerated pending trial. He was too great a flight risk, and people may act as sureties only in monetary matters, not criminal matters. The texts occasionally mention incarceration of a suspect. Apparently the incarceration was to keep the person available for the trial. No mention is made of long prison sentences. Penitentiaries as we know them date from the nineteenth century. In the period under notice only kings had dungeons in which (at best) to keep enemies of the state or indeed personal enemies.

In responsum 237 the author reverts to the matter of testimony and witnesses. One of the problems raised by Saul in *Ritba's* responsum was the legality of taking testimony outside the presence of the defendant. *Rivash* examines that point. *Rivash* first asserts that the decided law is that testimony is taken in the presence of the principal parties in any lawsuit. He then adduces a responsum of his great predecessor, *Rosh*, which holds that it is permissible to take testimony against an informer (the case referred to *Rivash* concerned an *alleged* informer) even if the accused is not present. *Rosh* contends that non-Jews will work with their Jewish informants. The non-Jews would keep him from harm. If it were necessary to take testimony against him in his presence, no case against an informer could ever go forward. The procedure in this sort of case is extraordinary — for maintaining public peace and order. *Rivash* goes on to say that should the judges in the case come to the conclusion that there is some circumstance warranting extraordinary procedure, the court should take the necessary steps to insure that justice is served in the long run. In sum, then, if necessary the accused need not be present when the witnesses are heard if good reason exists to believe that requiring his presence would in effect impede justice and let the guilty escape punishment.

None of the responsa that have detailed special measure jurisprudence has mentioned the composition of the court. Doubtless the actual composition varied from town to town. Saul apparently had one judge. Responsa are addressed to the leading personages of communities. Testimony in a blasphemy case which will be examined presently was taken by a court of three. The courts undoubtedly included a Rabbi if one was available and other learned and distinguished men, such as Don Judah Wakar.[13] The basic compliment for an ordinary rabbinic court is of course three, but in this period Spanish courts exhibited a variety of structures, although rabbinic opinion where pertinent was obviously sought.[14] The courts may have been composed of *adelantados* sitting as judges or selectmen (*berurim*) or other officers of the community appointed by the community to execute justice. When the local courts needed guidance on Jewish law, they reached out to the most eminent authorities available to them. No doubt they also addressed inquires to non-Jewish legal authorities when they required some enlightenment on the limit of their patents and on points of non-Jewish law. Above all, the courts of these medieval Jewish communities were charged to pursue justice for the welfare of the community, for the sake of Heaven and for the sanctification of the divine Name.

The punitive modalities for maintenance of public safety and order available to these Spanish communities ranged from capital punishment through various forms of corporal punishment, and flogging, down to fines and (probably brief) incarceration, excommunication and exile. The emphasis here has been on the most serious punitive modalities, because indeed they are the most serious, and reflect the harshest realities of a functioning legal system that faced and resolved genuine problems in public order and safety.

ASHKENAZIC COMMUNITIES

Not all Spanish communities enjoyed this range of power, and certainly Ashkenazic communities, the communities of northern and central Europe, possessed no such sweeping power. Yet those communities also experienced occasional homicidal outrages that threatened public peace and order. They too were always under the ever-watchful eye of non-Jewish overlords. We turn now to a case which offers the fullest illustration of punitive modalities available in an Ashkenazic environment.

In these communities there were no applications of special punitive mea-

13 See also below n. 19.
14 See Baer, *History of the Jews*, 1:212–16 and Epstein, *Responsa of Solomon b. Adret*, chap. 1, n.3.

sures supported by non-Jewish authority. The arsenal for suppression of threats to public order was far more modest. The most thorough rehearsal of what an Ashkenazic community was able to do in the face of a serious breach of peace comes from R. Israel b. Haim of Bruenn, a German authority of the fifteenth century.[15] In two responsa, 265 and 266 (ed. Salonika, 1798), he relates the story of a tavern brawl in which two Jews murdered a third. These two responsa are noteworthy for their detail though certainly homicide and informing occurred in the communities of Ashkenaz long before the fifteenth century.[16]

The responsa went to the community of Lemberg (Posen). It seems that one Nissan began a fight with Nahman and Simha. Nahman stabbed Nissan in the head, according to an eyewitness and also wounded the deceased so that he could not rise to his feet. Simha struck Nissan with a cudgel until Nissan was on the floor, dying, from his wounds.

One man deposed that Simha was drunk during this fracas and that Nissan was by no means a model citizen of the community; he was without even a veneer of piety. But when Simha had shown up sober the next morning, he was overcome with grief and remorse and sought to repent his evil deed. Nahman showed no such inclination.

R. Israel is in effect asked what the repentant murderer should do. The tone of his response echoes the rage he experienced upon receiving a trustworthy account of the tragic business. As far as he is concerned both men are stained with the guilt of murder even though the law, in *b.Sanh.* 78a, exempts them from answering to the human court since the law there speaks of murder committed by only one person and both men took a hand in the killing in the present case. Even so, they are still subject to a capital sentence decreed by a Divine Tribunal (*b.Ketub.* 30a, 30b).

R. Israel inveighs against the two of them, over and over, insisting that they are both murderers worthy of death. Yet he also notes the absence of the warning procedure required under the classic rules, and it is unclear from the report of the matter if there were in fact two competent witnesses under the classic rules. There certainly was no court of twenty-three ordained men to hear the case! However, no reference appears to a special measure or to the need of the hour. R. Israel was certainly as well aware of those texts as his Spanish colleagues of the previous century, but they simply could not be invoked since a capital penalty was out of the question and mutilation also never surfaces as an option in this case. That avenue was closed. The question was what to do within

15 Israel b. Haim of Bruenn, *Responsa of Israel b. Haim of Bruenn* (Salonika, 1798) nos. 265, 266.
16 An informer had after all caused the arrest and imprisonment of the great master R. Meir of Rothenburg in the thirteenth century. See Irving Agus, *Rabbi Meir of Rothenburg* (Philadelphia: Dropsie College, 1947). Though the work is over fifty years old, it is still the best treatment of R. Meir's work and career.

the strict boundaries of the Jewish law, absent any state license to impose capital or corporal punishment. Also no reference is found to non-Jewish involvement in the matter. Doubtless under non-Jewish laws of that time and place the two culprits should have gone to the gallows without too many complicated pre-liminaries, much to the chagrin of the Jews and (probably) to the amazement of the non-Jews. R. Israel obviously did not want to hand the accused men to non-Jewish authorities. One dead Jew was tragedy enough; three would have surely been unbearable. So, then, the question stands: how to punish them.

R. Israel alludes R. Eleazar of Worms (twelfth–thirteenth century, Rhineland) who received a tradition from his teacher R. Judah the Pious (twelfth–early-thirteenth century, Germany) concerning the procedure for a repentant mur-derer. The penalty involved exile from his home city for three years and the wearing of an iron band, plus other severe penalties. The full procedure, how-ever, is not given in detail. R. Israel chooses to be more lenient with Simha since he is at least thoroughly remorseful. He prescribes no procedure for Nahman until he should announce that he too repents of his murderous ways. Until he does so he shall be unfit to give any lawful testimony, take an oath, or be part of any quorum for a religious act.

R. Israel details a procedure of public repentance, humiliation, and public service as the proper penance for a person who has disturbed public order and safety in the Jewish community by an act of homicide. Responsum 266 pro-vides the general pattern which the scholars of Lemberg may modify if they see fit to do so.

First, Simha shall journey about as an exile for a full year. During that time he is to take an active part in the worship program of the community to which he travels. He is to go to synagogue every weekday or at least on every Monday and Thursday when the Torah is read publicly. He is to prepare three iron bands, one for each of his hands (or arms), which were the actual tools of the murder, and one to be worn around his body. He puts these bands on when he enters the syn-agogue to pray. In the evening he shall go to the synagogue barefoot. The haz-zan shall seat him (probably) prior to w'hu rachum, composed of Pss 78:38 and 20:10. This recitation occurs just before the formal call to worship. He shall then receive a public flogging (doubtless symbolic since an actual flogging of an in-determinate number of lashes would leave him dead sooner than later) and then declare, "Know ye, my masters, that I am a murderer. I wantonly killed Nissan. This is my atonement. Pray for me" (literally, "seek mercy for me"— the same word of course as in the immediately following w'hu rahum: "He is mer-ciful . . ."). When he leaves the synagogue, he is to prostrate himself upon the doorsill. The worshipers step over him, not on him. After this abasement he removes the iron bands for use the following day.

He is to fast every day for a full year except when tahanun is not recited in the morning liturgy. He is forbidden to eat meat or drink wine or strong spirits. He is to make certain he does not touch the liquor that he had on the occasion of the murder. Drunkenness contributed to his tragic act.

He may sleep on a soft bed only on Sabbaths and Holidays, including Hanukkah and Purim.

During the period of his exile from his home city he is not to cut or trim his hair or beard. He is forbidden to wash in hot water except on the eves of Sabbaths and Holidays. He may wash his hair once a month and his clothing, once every three months. The author's reference to bathing reflects the era in which these texts and cases arose.[17] These restrictions on personal hygiene appear a serious personal discomfort to the modern mind, and they surely are. Yet medieval standards of cleanliness were not high in any event so there may well be another aspect to this punishment. No one had "indoor running water" then and heating water involved pots and a fireplace or open fire. Every drop of water was procured from wells, rivers, streams, or springs and physically hauled in hand buckets or conveyed in a cart of some sort to dwellings or to the bath house, and then it was heated! The process was labor intensive. This miscreant, as repentant as he was, could not therefore make use of this precious resource for his own requirements except at special times when the honor of the occasion demanded it.

He is to stay away from taverns, since the killing occurred in a tavern; and he is forbidden to play games of chance, since the fatal argument began over such a game.

He is to recite the *Shema* and *Tefillah* portions of the liturgy with care and make the formal confession of sins thrice daily praying after each recitation for God to accept his repentance and declaring that his humiliation and shame are his atonement.

If people insult him with the epithet "murderer," he is simply to hold his peace and accept such insults meekly.

After a year of this regimen, Simha is to observe fasts on Mondays and Thursdays (unless they are religious festivals). He is to observe the anniversary of the killing. At that time he shall fast three consecutive days, two if he is ill, the day of the wounding itself and the next day, the actual day of the death.

For the rest of his life he shall be active in enterprises to free Jews incarcerated by non-Jews, charitable efforts and the saving of lives. He shall also work out some arrangement for the support of Nissan's heirs. He shall beg for their pardon for what he did. He shall return to God and God will have mercy on him.

---

17 The ordinary details of life which we take for granted were unknown to medieval Jewry. Hot water was a luxury. Cooking was a dangerous enterprise conducted over open fire using spits and pots. Fire was a frequent visitor to medieval towns, see below, "Protective Modalities," pp. 83–104.

R. Israel concludes his remarks with the observation that since Simha is remorseful and seeks atonement, once he accepts and enters upon the regimen of public repentance, humiliation, degradation, and work for the welfare of prisoners and the survivors of his victim, he once again becomes a Jew for every religious purpose: he may be part of a worship quorum. In this statement he follows the view of the tosafist R. Tam (*b.Bekh.* 31a s.v. *w'chulan shehazru*) although he himself says that he is not completely comfortable with that opinion. He simply accepts Rabbenu Tam's view for the present.

After hundreds of years the tones of outrage and sadness present in responsum 265 still resound with perfect clarity. Had there been some more severe penalty than the degradations, fasting, prayer regimen and the rest, which after all amounted to a life sentence to do good and utterly refrain from his former evils, it is not at all hard to image that R. Israel would have applied it to him. Presumably there was really nothing more punitive for him to employ. He does not mention fines or mulcts beyond what will be due to the heirs of his victim. He certainly does not entertain any notion of turning to the non-Jewish authorities for any assistance in imposing any punishments. That would certainly have heaped outrage upon outrage.

We do not know, however, whether or not Simha ever undertook all or any of the prescribed regimen. We only know what the Rabbi pronounced upon him, but nothing of his later career.

The arsenal of punition available to this authority lay entirely within the Jewish regimens of prayer, fasting, public humiliation, exile, and devotion to support the victim's survivors and other appropriate good works. The modalities actually available in Ashkenazic communities for the preservation of public peace and order were thus limited in matters of homicide in comparison with the special measures available in some Spanish communities. Yet the Ashkenazic regimens of fasting, prayer, humiliation, and the other elements of punition formed a life-long program for the accused to follow and fulfill. The key to the matter was of course the offender's degree of remorse, his willingness to accept such a program, and the resources of the community to ensure that he actually followed it. We have no information on these matters beyond the indications that Simha appeared remorseful and repentant, but Nahman did not. The modalities could be most effective in the punishment of a homicide if all parties were committed to following through with the prescribed several requirements.

BLASPHEMY

Homicide was apparently not the only threat to public order in Cordova. The communal leadership had addressed an inquiry to R. Asher b. Yehiel, R. Judah's illustrious father, the *Rosh*, about an incident of blasphemy which, if not swiftly and decisively handled, could have had serious consequences for the Jewish community.[18]

The essence of the events is as follows: The gentlemen of Cordova relate that a certain Jew, an egregious scoundrel, had been jailed over some claim a non-Jew brought against him. After striking some sort of compromise, he was released. Some acquaintances went to visit him and a conversation at the entry to his courtyard ensued. One visitor said, "Praised be He who frees the captive!" an utterance familiar from the daily liturgy. Thereupon that man turned his face heavenward cursing and blaspheming his King and his God. The judges and leading men of the community upon hearing of this untoward incident resolved to bring the man to trial for his blasphemy. They sent out to have him arrested, by what agency we are not told, but he was nowhere to be found.

They then attempted to take testimony against him outside his presence since he had fled, but they could find only one person to testify. The others who had been there were presumably incommunicado.

Don Judah b. Isaac Wakar, who acted as vice regent for Don Juan Manuel, then the regent of Castile, had secured for the Jewish community the authority to impose capital sentences.[19] That high official took an active interest in the case, and through the use of royal power had the accused found, arrested, and imprisoned. Similarly he used his influence to compel the missing witnesses to appear. He put them under oath and in proper manner took their testimony in the matter of the blasphemy.

Even though the blasphemy was uttered in Arabic (R. Asher relates that this scoundrel knew no Hebrew, had no Jewish education, had been a thorn in the side of the community for some time, and indeed no one had a good word for him), Don Judah and the judges and leading men of Jewish Cordova obviously agreed that his utterance should be deemed blasphemy. The noun for deity in Arabic, when uttered as he uttered it, is understood as blasphemy just as the Hebrew noun so used may constitute blasphemy. This decision was taken in order to *erect a barrier* in the matter lest the wicked and stupid become wanton in blasphemy presumably by using non-Hebrew terms. Clearly the Jews could not go about blaspheming in Arabic. That behavior would eventually become far more than embarrassing to the community! Blasphemy was a gross offense in the medieval world – Jewish, Christian or Moslem – and the Jew was in no position to anger a host community through such imprudent speech.

18 Asher b. Yehiel, *Responsa of Asher b. Yehiel* (Venice: Alvise Bragadini, 1552. New York: Grossman, 1954) no. 17:8.

19 This magnate had secured permission from Don Juan Manuel, Regent of Castile, for Jewish courts to judge capital cases. Don Juan was Christian, and Don Judah, Jewish; the blasphemy was in Arabic and doubtless at the time many Moslems still lived in the area of the event: a truly complex matter indeed.

While Don Judah and the Jewish leadership were busy with this decision to punish the offender, the man's relatives apparently bribed and requested the Regent Don Juan Manuel to delay the proceedings. He sent one of his knights to demand a delay in the action. R. Judah worked very hard on the matter. He placated the Regent that he not remove the matter from Jewish jurisdiction. The Jews should thus be seen as being willing and able to handle a matter of this gravity. They did not want it to go before a non-Jewish court. The accused was to remain in Don Judah's custody until Rosh's view of the case had been received.

The inquiry ends with a plea that the *Rosh* swiftly clarify matters and guide Don Judah in how to proceed before the matter is taken out of Jewish hands.

A copy of the testimony was appended to the documents. The testimony was taken in the presence of a court of three men who heard the testimony in the presence of others. The testimony was in Arabic. The responsum provides this transcription:

> Before us, the undersigned, R. Abraham b. Isaac testified that during the first five days of November . . . this witness went with R. Abraham Alzumi to R. Jacob b. Joseph Sefaya at the courtyard of R. Abraham b. Jacob Sefaya. Abraham Sefaya came out to meet them at the entrance to the courtyard. They greeted him and discussed the matter of Abraham Sefaya's incarceration. The witness said, "Praised be He who frees the prisoners . . .
>
> Abraham Sefaya thereupon said, "'Praised' be His name"— he pronounced this blessing after the fashion that the Sages have termed "blessing of The Name" (meaning a curse —"blessing" is used as irony. See *b.Sanh.* 56a). And the word which Abraham Sefaya uttered in this blasphemy was "May Allah bless" (that is, curse) in the Arabic language "so and so" and this "so and so" is the Name which is not proper to utter. Whereupon this witness said, "Praised be the True Judge" (a phrase from the funeral liturgy) "what are you saying?!" Abraham Sefaya responded, "Were it not that I prayed to Him this (incarceration) would not have happened to me.
>
> On this . . . day R. Abraham b. Isaac Alzumi testified to R. Jacob b. Joseph Sefaya the above noted version of this testimony which Abraham b. Nathan gave, but they were not absolutely certain that Abraham Sefaya used the divine Name in the blasphemy.

The *Rosh* responds in clear and decisive language. He provides firm direction for Don Judah. He remarks first how surprised he had been to find that in Spain Jews adjudicated capital cases, which did not occur in other Jewish areas of settlement. He notes that this jurisdiction is permitted under royal patent. He further notes that such an arrangement saves Jewish lives that would have been forfeit under non-Jewish law. He concludes this brief introductory paragraph with the statement that he personally never favored a capital punishment but he permitted the communities who had such power and authority to use it. That is, he did not interfere with the locally sanctioned practice in criminal matters.

The *Rosh* acknowledges that the community has resolved to purge the evil (person) from their midst. He has indeed uttered public blasphemy, and the matter has become known among the Moslems who are extremely strict with anyone who speaks against their religion and faith. Here of course is the link to public order and safety. Unless the matter is put to rest to the satisfaction of the larger non-Jewish community, the Jews could expect some form of trouble. Their lives were precarious enough without courting this sort of danger when they had the means to satisfy any potential enemy. *Rosh* endorses dealing with the accused according to the laws of the emergency measure. It is also only proper that the Divine Name be sanctified through the punishment.

The Bragadini edition of the responsum used here proceeds with Rosh's comment on the nature of the appropriate punishment. He says that if he were part of the inquirers' consensus, he would recommend that, rather than put the man to death, they should draw the tongue from his mouth and amputate the fore portion of it. He would be rendered dumb. By this form of punishment they would mete out to him measure for measure: he did wrong by spoken words; he shall *never* speak again. *Rosh* concludes that this vengeance is also manifest to the public at all times.

The non-Jewish community presumably would be placated by this severity, assuming that the person actually suffered it. In the event, one finds no indication of what actually occurred. What we do know and what may be surmised from both the inquiry and the response is that blasphemy was an offense that had serious potential for disturbing public order and safety. No punishment could be too severe. The Cordovans could put the man to death: *Rosh* did not allow his personal attitude to narrow the range of possible punishments. Yet even *Rosh*'s recommendation exhibits no lack of bloodletting. When their society as a whole faced a serious threat, the rabbinic authorities of Spain marshaled a full range of punitive modalities to suppress the wrongdoing.

SEXUAL IMPROPRIETY

Homicide and blasphemy clearly have the potential to disrupt public order, and the same is true for sexual liaisons in which Jews have non-Jewish partners. Although adultery and incest within the Jewish community prompted swift and condign punishment when and as it could be established, obviously such offenses were conducted in secrecy; and if any witnesses were present, they undoubtedly tended to be family members of the participants. At least the problem was something within the community and could be handled internally. The matter of liaisons outside the community was something else. They had potential to upset the peaceful balance of society. These liaisons were not just against Jewish law, they were against Muslim law or Christian law as well. Communities had to take steps to stop such behavior before the community might suffer because of the sins of one Jew. Two responsa, again from Spanish masters, suggest the sort of extreme measures incidents of such license could evoke.

A CASE OF SEXUAL LICENSE

Once again we examine a *responsum* from R. Judah b. Asher.[20] It deals with a case of sexual license in which a Jewish man had a sexual liaison (or liaisons?) with non-Jewish women. He prefaces his assessment of the case itself with a powerful endorsement of the authority of the local court to maintain public order and safety. He asserts the reason that the Jewish court adjudicates capital cases is two-fold: defendants tried under non-Jewish laws might well be sentenced to death while under Jewish law they would not face a death penalty; and conversely under Jewish law certain persons, informers against Jewish lives or property, can be put to death while under non-Jewish law they would not face such a penalty, or perhaps not be tried at all.[21]

He goes on: In every generation special measures become necessary to curb dissolute behavior among the people. The court is entrusted with the power and authority to carry out this work, and they do so as it seems proper for them to wall off the breach in Jewish propriety. He cites *b.Sanh.* 46a, the key text in such matters, declaring that every court dedicated to the sacred duty of establishing proper justice has the authority to flog and otherwise punish according to the need of the time. This punishment will serve as an example to others: they will hear of what happened to the offender and fear to receive similar treatment, even though the person's offense was not so great that the guilty person was worthy of such severe punishment. Thus, a punitive modality may be out of proportion to the offense punished, and no hint is found of any moral concern over excessive severity. The public must have a powerful object lesson so that it may repair its ways. The practical effectiveness of such an approach is similarly not explored: does it really serve the purpose?

He comes next to the specific matter of the man's sexual liaison with a

20 Judah b. Asher, *Responsa Zichron Yehudah*, no. 63.
21 The power of Jewish courts to try capital matters in some Spanish communities obviously cut both ways. On one hand Jews could protect themselves from the informer in their midst; on the other hand, by having such jurisdiction they could protect people from a gentile death sentence in certain sorts of cases — as long as presumably there was some punishment that satisfied Spanish authorities. This fascinating subject however stands over for the present.

non-Jewish woman. His punishment is really a matter for divine justice, not the human court, once the act has occurred. At the moment of the transgression, however, he may be put to death by the zealots after the manner of Pinhas who killed Zimri (Num 25:6–9). But divine justice will not apparently do to satisfy the world of the here and now in fourteenth-century Spain. The author presents another, less vague, procedure. He writes that in order for a generation not to become dissolute in sexual license and a Jew not be endangered by such a liaison with a non-Jewish woman, it is therefore proper for every court to punish one who transgresses in this manner, in such a fashion that the breach be repaired and danger to others averted.

The type of punishment depends on the wrongdoer.[22] For some, the court's solemn warning to cease and desist from such activity may suffice, and if it does not he may be remanded to civil authority to face whatever fate they may have in store for him. That will surely put a stop to the behavior. If it appears that he is able to restrain himself, well and good! If the court determines that he cannot act with restraint after its warning, he may be required to leave the city; in this way, of course, the people of that place are no longer in danger, but that is hardly comforting to a neighboring Jewish community. If the court determines that a warning will be of no avail in the first place, then they immediately exile him from the city and indeed from all the provinces of the Prince. Or the court may take such other punitive steps as may seem appropriate, so that the offense and the danger from it are removed. In any event, so long as no well established case against the man exists, that is, there is insufficient evidence for a Jewish court to act, and he does not have a clear idea of the possible consequences of his behavior – his only remedy is "the grave!"– the man's person shall not be harmed. The insistence on keeping the person physically unharmed no doubt accounts for no further mention of any remand to non-Jewish authorities. That is only a threat, at least as long as no solid case can be made against him or as long as non-Jewish authorities are not tipped off to the matter. What is clear from this text is that the court enjoys wide latitude to warn or expel men who may endanger the welfare of the Jewish community through their pursuit of non-Jewish women. A man was given a chance to restrain himself or else he had to leave. The case of the woman reflects a less benign approach to this sort of matter.

A SECOND CASE OF SEXUAL LICENSE

A second case of sexual license, this time concerning a Jewish woman and a non-Jewish man, comes from the pen of the *Rosh*, 18:13. He dealt with the case

---

22 See Hershman, *Rabbi Isaac b. Sheshet Perfet*, 128–36 and chap. 14 on Informers.

of a Jewish widow who had become pregnant by a Moslem man. She admitted the affair and had even signed over property to the man. The inquirer had conducted an investigation into the matter but found no one who could give any reliable testimony on the matter. The situation had become "common knowledge" in town.

Further it seems that the Moslems brought a complaint on this matter before Don Juan, but he told them that the case was out of his hands because the woman is a Jew. It further turned out that the woman gave birth to twins, a boy and a girl. The male infant died, and she converted the infant girl to Islam.

The inquirer then earnestly seeks *Rosh*'s guidance because he took it as a divine sign that Don Juan refused to rule in the matter, leaving it in Jewish hands. Thus he wants to know how he should rule so that Jewish law will not suffer a public disgrace. He proposes to deal as harshly as possible with the woman. The case of this whore (the inquirer's term) has become infamous in the area and Judaism has become despised among non-Jews. Also Jewish women would take note of an object lesson and not follow in her footsteps.

The inquirer suggests that the woman suffer "disfigurement of the face" which she beautified for her lover and also be required to pay a sum of money to the city. The edition of the responsum by Grossman (1954) simply mentions disfigurement.[23] The text of the responsum as cited by R. Joseph Karo in *Bet Yosef* to *Tur, Hoshen Mishpat*, chapter 2 is more graphic. That text describes the disfigurement of the face as amputation of the nose.

The inquiry concludes by asking the *Rosh* if he concurs in this suggestion or if he has something perhaps more severe in mind. He will follow whatever *Rosh* advises. The inquirer subscribes himself Don Judah Wakar, indeed the same gentleman we encountered in the case of blasphemy which *Rosh* decided.

Rosh's response is only a few lines. He heartily concurs in the suggested course of action Don Judah proposes. Her face should be mutilated, and this should be done quickly that she not convert. Her wealth should be assessed and the fine levied accordingly.

Obviously if the woman became a Moslem she would no longer be subject to Jewish law. The public disgrace of Judaism which Don Judah senses would continue; Judaism would become a laughingstock.

One finds no indication whether or not the woman actually suffered the frightful penalty prescribed by Don Judah and approved by *Rosh*. Yet a penalty uninflicted is no penalty at all; in this situation, the better presumption is that the Jewish court would have imposed this cruel penalty if it were at all possible to do so. It is indeed a most terrible punishment in itself and it becomes even

23 *Responsa of R. Asher b. Yehiel*, 18:13.

more stark when compared with the mere warning and the expulsion that a promiscuous man might suffer.

The woman would surely have become an object lesson to all other Jewish women, and possibly the threat of such terrible punishment could have had a contrary and unintended effect. At least one husband may have had an idea of the possible consequences of his wife's adultery with a non-Jew and become complicit in a cover-up of her promiscuity when he came home to a scene that appeared far from innocent.[24] In the present case, however, the fact of the advanced pregnancy and the public awareness of the liaison provoked a penalty of great severity.

The Jews clearly treasured their power and authority to maintain order and safety in their communities, To that end, their law could not be held up to disgrace or ridicule, nor could their people have any doubts as to the consequences of flouting it.

The Jewish communities of Spain possessed no more powerful modality for the maintenance of public order and public safety than the "emergency measure," backed by royal license; not even excommunication, a modality which will be examined later on, could hold the same terrors. Excommunication could after all be lifted; the consequences of the emergency measure were all too permanent: death or mutilation. When local judges resolved to protect the public welfare by imposing an emergency measure, they presumably took counsel with the wisest and most learned in their immediate locality; and they certainly reached out to solicit expert rabbinical opinion if they had any doubt about the legality or propriety of what they intended to do. The texts also make it quite clear that the judges had to approach their task with the sole purpose of seeing justice done, of acting for the sake of Heaven, unalloyed by any base and unworthy consideration.

MAYHEM AND BATTERY

Homicide, blasphemy and sexual misconduct were the more serious acts which threatened the peace and good order of Jewish communities, but not the only ones. The focus now shifts to another source of such threats: mayhem and battery. No society can endure for very long if its members are able to hurt and pummel each other without fear of punishment. Modalities existed for the preservation of peace and order that could be brought to bear when cases of mayhem and battery came before Jewish courts. The attempt here is to examine those modalities which actually appear to have operated in the medieval Jewish legal system, not necessarily the classic rules of the Mishnah and Gemara.

---

24 See above, n. 7, Passamaneck, "Remarks on Pesquisa," 150–51. The matter looks much like a *pesquisa*.

THREE OR FOUR MODALITIES

The Hebrew Bible presents three and possibly four modalities for the punishment of mayhem and aggravated battery. Exodus 21:18, 19 provides that a person injured in an attack, whether or not the attack involved a weapon, shall be reimbursed by his attacker for medical expenses and time lost from work. If the victim is the attacker's slave, who loses an eye or a tooth in the attack, or presumably any other major body part, the slave is to be freed (Exod 21:26, 27). In the biblical discussion of the pregnant woman who miscarries as a consequence of a fight between two men, the woman's husband shall take the injurer to court where the judge will determine the fine the attacker is to pay (Exod 21:22). The passage goes on to state that if "any harm follows," that is, if the woman should die, a capital penalty may apply, "life for life"; then follows one of the most famous passages of the Hebrew Bible: "an eye for an eye, a tooth for a tooth, hand for hand, foot for foot, burning for burning, wound for wound, stripe for stripe" (Exod 21:23–25). The subject of mayhem and battery reappears in Deut 25:11 in the case of the woman who rescues her husband by grabbing the testicles of the man attacking him. She is to suffer the loss of her hand for this act. Finally Deut 17:8–13 speaks to the matter of a case that is too difficult for the local judge to decide. This could, by extension, include a case of mayhem or aggravated battery too complex for local judges to handle. Such a case is to be referred to a court which is presumably more learned and experienced which will resolve the case and impose the proper sentence and punishment.

The three clear punitive modalities are money payments, retaliation by the court, freedom in the case of a slave, and possibly the unpredetermined sentence of a higher court, charged to handle difficult cases. The person who wounds his slave need not detain us. Slavery had long since disappeared from the Jewish community as a frequent phenomenon in the Middle Ages and certainly questions involving slaves, much less the grievous wounding of one, simply did not arise. Slavery as a living phenomenon had long ceased to exist by the period under notice here. The other modalities require some consideration.

MONEY PAYMENTS

By the time of the Mishnah, punishment by retaliation, limb for limb, had been transformed into a series of money payments (*m.B.Qam.* 8:1). These rules form the classic program for dealing with mayhem and aggravated battery. They are as much the classic rules for this area of concern as the material in *Sanhedrin* and *Makkot* is for homicide.

The offender had to pay a series of fines. The court assessed one amount for depreciation: the person is considered as if he (or she) were a slave, and a determination is made of the person's before-injury value and after-injury value.

The difference is payable to the victim and was presumably the largest of the several assessments since it contemplates the depreciation of the victim's value over his or her working life. An amount was assessed for pain: how much would a person of the victim's standing demand in order to experience that degree of pain. An amount is payable for medical expenses, but only for medical expenses due to the specific injury, for as long as the injury is not fully healed. A sum is payable for loss of time. The victim is deemed employable as a low wage worker in a job a lame person can hold. He receives the wages for that position, not his previous employment, since the value of his lost limb has already been calculated for him and that sum would cover the much larger amount of the person's "value" with respect to the occupation he or she could no longer pursue. An amount is payable for "degradation," which is calculated on the basis of the social standing of the offender and the offended. The woman who rescued her husband (Deut 25:11) does not lose her hand for inflicting degradation on the attacker; she pays an amount for the embarrassment she caused by inflicting that painful indignity (b.B.Qam. 28a).

A person committing mayhem or aggravated battery might be required to pay all five sums or some lesser number of them depending on the circumstances of the case. Although the gemara to m.B.Qam. 8:1 (b.B.Qam. 83b–87a) examines the several payments, it never mentions any specific money amount that was payable in an actual case.

The fourth possible punitive modality, a special sort of court that would decide a difficult case and impose the correct punishment, is always an option of course, although none of the medieval cases we shall examine make any reference to it. It is, so to speak, a catch-all category that is also apparently a sort of judicial device for emergency measures for the need of the hour, though no claim to any sort of direct relationship is to be inferred. There is only a possibility. The cases we shall look at came before regular courts of the Jewish community. The idea that special cases call for special treatment no doubt emerges in every historical period, including our own.

In any event, the clearly preferred punitive modality for mayhem and aggravated battery in the period of the Talmud was some sort of pecuniary compensation, although R. Huna, as we have seen, was quite willing to impose amputation of the hand upon one persistent batterer. These cases have thus become diné mammonot, pecuniary cases. These sums, as has been mentioned, are considered fines in the halakhah, although they are payable to the victim, not to any "governmental agency."

So far, the subject has been mayhem and aggravated battery, clearly major disruptions of public safety and order. There are, however, batteries of lesser severity, and those as well are discussed in the Babylonian Talmud; b.B.Qam. 27b and 90a give a list of such batteries and of the amounts of money the court will oblige the offender to pay his victim. These batteries do not cause permanent injury, and no lasting discomfort, but they are embarrassing and upsetting. They form another set of "classic" rules:

> If one kicked another with his foot, he pays five *sela*'s.
>
> If one kicked another with his knee, three *sela*'s.
>
> A blow with a closed fist, 13 *sela*'s.
>
> A slap with an open hand, one *sela*'.
>
> If the slap is to the face, 50 *sela*'s.
>
> A backhanded slap to the face, 100 *sela*'s.
>
> If a blow split the victim's ear, or the attacker pulled the victim's hair, or spat upon exposed skin, 100 *sela*'s.

All of these amounts are considered fines and are intended to reimburse for pain, embarrassment, medical costs (even if no treatment is necessary) and time lost from work. One can easily imagine any of these batteries as the climax of a shouting match, and the delivery of a kick or blow is the signal for a friend or bystanders to separate the antagonists. Doubtless these minor batteries were far more frequent than cases of mayhem.

The classic rules involve fines, and that causes a problem because only judges ordained in the Land of Israel were deemed competent to adjudicate cases of fines. Just as cases of homicide required such ordained judges, so too did cases of fines. The disqualification of judges outside the Land of Israel with respect to assessing and imposing fines appears as an unquestioned presumption embedded in an extended talmudic discussion (*b.B.Qam.* 84a–b). The fourth-century Amora Rava is said to hold that payment for physical injury inflicted by one person upon another is not adjudicated by judges in Babylonia, that is, outside the Land of Israel. The discussion probes for the reason underlying this position. The term *Elohim*, appearing in the Hebrew Bible, for example, Exod 21:6, in the sense of judges, does not apply to the Babylonian masters of the law. Yet in another utterance of *Elohim* as judges, Babylonian masters do handle such cases, acting so to speak as the "agents" of the Palestinian masters in these and other matters of judgment. Why then in these cases of fines should they not similarly function as "agents" of the ordained men? There is an attempt to explain the absence of agency on the basis of the nature of the payment involved: if the payment is a fixed matter, the Babylonians may undertake agency, but not if it requires "valuation" — an assessment involving a judgment call. The talmudic discussion proceeds: this explanation is not acceptable because the Babylonians do assume agency in matters involving valuation as when an animal has to be valued in the marketplace. And there are moreover cases in which clearly established amounts of payment are *not* adjudicated by Babylonians: the biblical four-fold and five-fold payments. The response to this point is that Babylonians handle pecuniary matters involving a "civil liability," but not in penal matters like fines as in four-fold and five-fold payments. A case involving money is one thing, a case involving a fine, a penalty element, is quite something else; and judges outside of Israel have no jurisdiction in them. Yet the matter of injury inflicted by one person upon another docs not necessarily involve a penal element; a person has been "reduced in value," a plain matter of money payment! This is met with the assertion that the Babylonian masters assumed agency for the ordained Palestinians only in cases that are rather frequent, but mayhem and battery were not considered frequent occurrences.

Finally the matter of embarrassment or "degradation" is adduced. This aspect of "injury" to a person is rather frequent so why cannot the Babylonian authorities serve as the "agents" of the Palestinians in this respect? Indeed the Babylonian, R. Papa (fourth century) ordered payment for embarrassment. R. Papa's case, however, is not accepted by the *gemara* as a valid model because R. Hisda (Babylonia late third, early fourth century) consulted his Babylonian contemporary, R. Nahman, a renowned scholar of rabbinic jurisprudence, who questioned R. Hisda and expressed surprise and incredulity that R. Hisda appeared ready to order payment of a fine in Babylonia. The presumption that it is *not* done is a constant theme in the entire extended discussion. The conclusion reached in the *gemara* is that Babylonian authorities may function as the "agents" of the ordained masters of Palestine only in matters that occur frequently and which involve actual monetary loss. The matter of "embarrassment" is indeed frequent, but it entails no actual financial loss, as the rabbis understand matters, while mayhem and battery are simply not frequent. Thus, the judges outside the Land of Israel do not handle fines and therefore are not qualified to sit on cases of mayhem and battery.

Certainly cases of mayhem and battery, particularly the less severe types of battery, occurred in the talmudic period, perhaps even frequently. People being what they are, arguments come to blows. It is impossible that a large and active community in constant contact with each other could not have experienced such events. We do not, however, have any record of how they were actually decided, and probably most of them never got to court!

Several possibilities exist for those that did. Perhaps other judges acted after the fashion of R. Papa and awarded sums to victims even though that was, strictly speaking, unlawful. Perhaps the rabbinic court put the offender under an excommunicatory ban, a coercive measure until the offender came to some agreement with the victim over costs and values of limbs and the like. Perhaps the courts developed some creative measures to make up for the absence of actual jurisdiction. Perhaps public pressure on the offender, even without excommunication, was sufficient to effect some sort of equitable resolution to the matter. The fact is that we do not know exactly what happened, what modalities emerged. And again, the likelihood is that most cases of cuffs and punches were resolved by the antagonists themselves without judicial intervention.

THE POST TALMUDIC PERIOD

When we look at the post talmudic period we clearly perceive the emergence of modalities for treating mayhem and battery that medieval authorities employed. These probably involved the more serious or infamous cases.

Precisely this problem of fines in battery came to the attention of R. Zemah Gaon, a late ninth-century Gaon at Sura.[25] He wrote a response to the question of whether or not fines were collectable so that a "sinner should not be rewarded." The idea of course is that without some modality to deal with mayhem and battery, the individual offender would benefit and society would suffer.

His answer was that it is a general talmudic principle that Jewish courts do not collect fines outside of Palestine. He cites the *b.B.Qam.* 27b passage noted above and simply states that we follow Rava's view that we do not collect the damages occasioned by injury inflicted by one person upon another. He, however, continues: so that the offender not be rewarded (*b.Ketub.* 11a) and Jews not become unrestrained in matters of mayhem and battery, since Jews will know that the fines for such offenses will not be payable outside Palestine, he informs us that the later sages adopted a specific practice to meet the problem. They instituted an excommunicatory ban against the offender to last until he should be reconciled with his victim, whether by mutually acceptable money payment or through the agency of friends speaking on his behalf. R. Zemah Gaon relates an incident in which one man knocked out the tooth of another man. The case had come before R. Zemah's late predecessor at Sura, R. Zadok Gaon. He said to the offender that he could not impose a fixed penalty on him, but that he should go and effect reconciliation with the victim, whether through money or "words" (or presumably both!). R. Zemah concludes his responsum by declaring that nowadays when fines are no longer imposed and collected, the practice of R. Zadok Gaon has become the accepted practice.

Substantially the same responsum is also found in the name of R. Natronai Gaon, also a master of Sura in the late ninth century.[26] Two versions of it exist. In the first one there is the statement that the fines for mayhem and battery are not collected in Babylonia or in any other place outside of Palestine. R. Zadok's case is cited. R. Zadok's procedure was instituted so that Jews not go

---

25 See Benjamin M. Lewin, *Otzar Hageonim, Bava Qamma* (Jerusalem: Mossad Harav Kuk, 1943).
26 Lewin, *Otzar Hageonim.*

around wounding each other; the text declares that it has become the standard procedure in the courts. The second version also asserts that fines are not collectible in Babylonia or other places outside of Palestine, but if a victim has seized property of the offender we do not require him to surrender it. R. Zadok's case is again cited as the procedure to prevent Jews from indulging in mayhem and battery. Neither of the two versions attributed to Natronai Gaon mention the element of the coercive ban.

What happened in such matters prior to the time of R. Zadok is not discussed, but presumably something along the lines of R. Zadok's practice would probably have been followed. Any other procedure would have elicited some remark. R. Zadok's case was simply the classic ruling in this type of case for which we have a halakhic notation.

The modality is thus a combined one: a coercive ban that is coupled with a court order to the offender to reconcile with the victim either through money payment or through persuasion carried out by the offender himself or by friendly intermediaries. No doubt both types of reconciliation were present in any given case and the amount of money involved would have been large or small depending on the nature of the injury or injuries inflicted.

R. Solomon b. Adret, *Rashba,* whom we have already met, takes up the matter of fines, and by implication, cases of mayhem and battery, in a responsum about the legality of testimony before a court of *beruré averoth*, selectmen for the purging of wrongdoing in the community.[27] In paraphrase, the enquirer first explains that the Jewish community agreed to appoint *beruré averoth* in their town to purge wrongdoing. Included in the details of the agreement was that the community would exercise authority, under governmental license, to inflict punishment, whether bodily or financial as they see fit. The enquirer then gets down to cases; he asks, if witnesses related to R., who had violated his oath, testified against him, and those witnesses appear credible, or if a woman and a minor speak in all innocence and are quite ignorant of the impact their statements may have on R.'s case, may the court then punish R. on the basis of such testimony? Does the court have the authority to accept and act upon such testimony or not, even though there is no absolutely unequivocal and irrefutable testimony against R.?

Rashba responds that the matter appears quite straightforward to him. The community is authorized to do what appears proper to it. The questions raised about disqualification of witnesses only arise in courts which function according to classic Torah law. But a court based upon the regulations of the territory does not function according to actual Torah law, rather it proceeds according to

27 On the *beruré averot*, see Stephen M. Passamaneck, "The Beruré Averot and the Administration of Justice in XIII and XIV Century Spain," *Jewish Law Association Studies* 4 (1990) 135–46. *Responsa of R. Solomon b. Adret*, 4:311.

what is required by the times, under governmental permit. Were that not so, no punishments, corporal or financial, could be imposed since "fines are not collectable in Babylonia," nor could we adjudicate infrequently occurring matters, since we do not adjudicate them, even in matters of loans, according to classic Torah law.[28] *Rashba* proceeds: we do act as agents of the Palestinian authorities in frequently arising cases, such as admittances and loans. In infrequently arising matters such as robbery and wounding and other such wrongdoings, we do not presume to act as agents. Therefore a person is not to be flogged or punished in his property on his own testimony, since a person cannot condemn himself to punishment out of his own mouth, according to Torah law. Even if there are fully qualified witnesses against him, there shall be no corporal punishment unless the court had previously issued a formal warning to the offender.

After thus briefly reviewing the technical grounds which preclude the effective functioning of Jewish law as a program for achieving criminal justice, *Rashba* does a turn about. All that discussion applies only to a court that functions according to *Torah law*. He then cites the incident in which David ordered the death of the Amalekite man who had given Saul his quietus on the battlefield. David ordered the death of the man presumably because the time required it, so that the offense of killing the "Lord's anointed" would not be overlooked and unpunished. *Rashba* cites as further substantiation that some matters have to be decided according to the need of the hour, the situation envisaged in *b.Yebam.* 90b that records the special measures taken to safeguard Torah, as the need of the hour required even if that need led to a flogging or a death penalty.

His final word to his questioner allays any fears that the community was acting unlawfully. The entire proposal of the communal agreement was to make certain that wrongdoing was properly punished and suppressed. That is the key, and therefore according to *Rashba* the matter is simple and straightforward. The responsum does not mention a punitive modality as such. It simply leaves the door open to whatever modality may seem appropriate in the case under consideration.

The range of modalities was certainly clear to the Spanish masters. They could follow the example of the Geonim with reconciliation and money payment. They could flog or otherwise punish under a local ordinance adopted by this or that community. Indeed Saul, whom we met above, complained that he should have been held to answer under the terms of a local ordinance and not suffer amputation. They could institute a ban against the offender until he made good a pecuniary judgment against him. Or, they could honor a

---

28 See above pp. 54, 55 for the review of the talmudic discussion regarding the permissibility of imposing fines outside the land of Israel.

page from R. Huna's book and order amputation. A range of modalities was available to the Spanish communities that exercised criminal jurisdiction under royal license, and every such modality was arguably perfectly licit under Jewish law as they practiced it.

The Spanish communities did not have a monopoly on cases of wounding and battery. The Ashkenazic authorities also had to have procedures to curb and punish disruptions of the public peace. *Rashba*'s illustrious Ashkenazic contemporary, R. Meir of Rothenberg (d. 1293), provides a glimpse or two into the modalities he applied when faced with cases of battery.[29]

In the first responsum we encounter a jarring streak of violence. R. Meir seems non-plussed. S. grabbed a person by the neck, pulled a knife on him and said, "I'll cut your head. . . ." R. Meir is at a loss for words. He says that the man indeed performed a wicked and shameful act. He notes that Jewish courts no longer adjudicate cases of wounding according to classic Jewish law, but individual communities customarily enact local ordinances to cover such matters. If the community where this occurred imposed a fine, that local procedure is to be followed. The fine is the only specific modality R. Meir applies to this case. Local option is to be followed.

He then makes a more general statement. All rabbis have concurred that one who raises his hand against another is deemed wicked and is unfit to act as a witness or to swear an oath until he makes public repentance – this is for the one who raises his hand yet does not strike a blow – how much the more for the one who grabs another, raises his fist and threatens him with a knife! R. Meir then remarks that if the event had occurred in his town he would have had the offender flogged.

There is in effect a suggestion that a combination of modalities may be in order. The local fine for one thing, the public manifestation of repentance, and even a flogging. R. Meir comments on a case of wife beating (responsum 81). He rehearses the talmudic demand that a Jew is duty bound to honor his wife more than he does himself; he is not to harm her. He quotes from the standard wedding contract document: "he is to honor and support her." He cites a tradition that a judge shall deal more severely with a wife beater than with an ordinary batterer. He adds that wife beating is a non-Jewish behavior, and God forbid that any Jewish man should do this. One who does this should be placed under an excommunicatory ban, flogged, and suffer all types of punishments, even the amputation of his hand if he frequently beats his wife, as R. Huna authorized in his talmudic case of battery. R. Meir then widens the scope of the possible modalities. He writes that even though cases of fines are not

---

29 Meir ben Baruch, *Responsa of R. Meir of Rothenburg* (Prague, Budapest: Sternberg & Co., 1895) nos. 81, 383.

adjudicated, severe penalties may be imposed outside Palestine so that men do not treat this matter lightly. He concludes this portion of the responsum with the suggestion that if she wishes a divorce, the husband is to divorce her and pay her wedding settlement.

R. Meir significantly expands the list of modalities previously suggested to include the amputation of the offender's hand if the offenses have been repeated. Whether or not this punishment was a real option in the Jewish community is unexplored. He clearly has no patience with wife beaters and would bring the full pressure of the law against them.

We turn next to two more Ashkenazic authorities, R. Jacob Weil and R. Israel Isserlein, both fifteenth-century figures renowned among German Jewish rabbinic scholars. Rabbi Jacob Weil commented on a case of battery with wounding.[30] The case again reminds us that threats to public safety and order did not always come from outside the Jewish community. There was some home-grown violence as well as the external threat of violence from the non-Jewish world. The home-grown variety could not of course be tolerated.

The situation appears to be thus: R. seeks redress from S. because S. struck him on the head, giving him a bloody wound. One witness says that he saw S. hit R. and cause a bleeding head wound. Another witness says he saw S. run after R. and give him the bloody wound. S. admits that he did so but only after R. had struck S.'s wife. S. became enraged and gave him the wound. From the testimony it appeared that S. struck R. prior to R.'s attack on S.'s wife.

R. Weil castigates S. who has committed a grave offense. He cites *b.Sanh.* 58b that condemns the batterer; and, in the opinion of Resh Lakish (Palestine, third century C.E.), even the person who would raise his hand against another without delivering a blow is wicked indeed. R. Huna has the offender's hand amputated. R. Eleazar declares with massive hyperbole the batterer has no remedy save the grave.

If then the person who only threatens to batter is so severely punished, how much more the person who actually delivers a blow and causes a bloody wound. R. Weil adds further detail about the incident: "How much the more does the offender here deserve severe punishment because he grabbed a piece of wood with his two hands, struck R. on the head, a dangerous place for a severe wound, and the blood poured out. He hit him with all his strength! He was not concerned that he might cause a mortal injury." He characterizes the injury as a "merciless wound."

R. Weil also writes that it further appears R. was an elderly man, which only compounds the battery with the offense of gross disrespect for the aged. He

30 Jacob b. Judah Weil, *Responsa of Jacob Weil* (Jerusalem: Safra, 1959) no. 28.

at length declares that S. shall be unfit to give testimony or to swear an oath until he shall make public repentance for his sins. In the case under notice the offender shall also be flogged, that he never again raise his hand to another person. R. Weil mentions a responsum in his possession concerning a person who grabbed another Jew by the throat, pulled a knife on him, and threatened to cut his head (R. Meir's responsum). All authorities agreed that this battery at the least — and it is certainly battery — coupled with a possibly deadly threat should render the batterer unfit to give testimony or swear an oath until he shall have made public repentance for his sin, even though he did not carry out the threat. The responsum R. Weil cites concludes with the dire pronouncement that if the incident had occurred in his (that is, R. Meir's) community, he would have ordered a flogging. If flogging is deemed proper where the deed is not done, how much the more when it was done!

R. Weil goes on to quote R. Judah Hehasid: the batterer shall publicly seek the victim's pardon and receive a flogging because he struck the victim. In the present case, therefore, R. Weil declares that no one would dispute the propriety of a flogging. The offender shall go to synagogue on Monday and Thursday, ascend the *bimah* after the reading of Torah and announce in a loud voice that he has sinned. He is required to recount the specific elements of his offense and ask for divine forgiveness and pardon from his victim. He is further required on that same day to attend synagogue and to be present there between the afternoon and the evening worship services, at which time he will be flogged, prior to the recitation of the "*w'hu rahum.*" R. Weil concludes the recitation of the punishment by requiring the offender to pay the victim a sum of money. The transgression will thus be expiated.

R. Weil is not certain about how much money is to be paid. Clearly it is a fine and just as clearly he is not at all concerned with the matter of collecting a fine outside the Land of Israel. He does relate that he heard of a case of battery in which the Rabbi deciding the case ordered the offender to pay a third of all his property, but he has no information on the substance of that matter. He therefore declines to use it as a precedent for his own action in R.'s case. He suggests that if R. is a poor man then S. shall give him a silver mark; if R. is wealthy, S. shall give the silver mark to those who labor in Torah, that is to a fund for the support of scholars.

R. Weil adds a final note to S.'s list of punishments. After S. shall have fulfilled the demands of his punishment he shall once again be deemed qualified to give testimony and swear an oath. As for the sum of a "silver mark," this, says the author, is the prescribed sum only if there is no established custom as to fines for batterers in the questioner's district. If such an established custom exists, it is to be followed.

R. Weil's responsum presents modalities for battery, and battery with wounding, similar to those imposed for homicide in places where the Jews did not exercise capital jurisdiction. One finds the public assertion of guilt and the plea for pardon. There is flogging and there is a money payment. Simcha, the intoxicated murderer whom we met earlier, faced the same penalties although the money he paid was in the form of settlement or support for the victim's survivors. In the case of battery the money goes to the victim, and the sum involved may or may not be dictated by local custom or ordinance. It is not in any case identified as a classic fine which all authorities would agree is simply not collectable outside the Land of Israel and which requires ordained judges, who no longer existed anywhere. The one element that is not included in R. Weil's list is the excommunicatory ban, but it is not mentioned in the case of the homicide either.

The final responsum in this section on punitive modalities comes from another of the great Ashkenazic authorities of the fifteenth century, R. Israel Isserlein of Wiener Neustadt.[31] We come once again to a special court-ordered measure as a punitive modality. The situation is clearly an egregious breach of public peace and order.

Two men, Eliezer and Gershom, inveterate enemies, appeared before R. Isserlein. Eliezer charged that Gershom had pushed and shoved him during the *hoshana* circuits at the Sukkot festival, intending to injure him. Eliezer had been shoved so violently that he suffered a broken shoulder and required medical attention. Gershom said that he participated in the circuits in the usual manner, when there is customarily a good deal of jostling. He claims that if he did any shoving, it certainly was not with the intention of causing bodily harm.

R. Isserlein carefully reviewed the testimony but did not find any clear proof that Gershom had intentionally injured Eliezer, although there were plausible indications that he did so. One witness testified that on the night prior to the event Gershom had said to him that he was of a mind to give Eliezer a shove on the morrow, and when Gershom was leaving the synagogue after the unfortunate event, Gershom had asked him why the witness had not helped Eliezer when he was pushed. This was the clearest evidence of Gershom's intentional involvement in the battery.

R. Isserlein does not believe this is sufficient evidence to establish guilt under Torah law. What was said the night before may be dismissed as a mere boast and a person may utter a boast and not carry it out (*b.Šebu.* 46a). Further, as to what Gershom said as he was leaving the synagogue, that was merely an unwitnessed utterance out of court and not in the presence of his adversary. It is not acceptable as reliable testimony. The author therefore argues that one may not attri-

31 Israel Isserlein, *Responsa of R. Israel Isserlein*, sec. 2, *Pesaqim U'ketabim* (ed. Venice, 1519) no. 210.

bute guilt on the basis of plausibility and indications alone (*b.B.Bat.* 93a). In the case before him, he would need a good many indications that Gershom acted with criminal intent. If he did not intend to cause injury, even though he surely did do so, he would in this situation be held exempt from any punishment since the act occurred during the performance of a religious obligation!

R. Isserlein is not at all satisfied with the conclusion at which he arrived according to the law and the evidence. He declares that this sort of an incident demands a major protective measure, since people could lie in wait for each other at the time of the circuits and thus that religious duty would then be neglected out of fear of injury from one's enemies. An injury inflicted at such a time and place is in his opinion worse than the same injury inflicted at another time and place. The sanctity of the synagogue is sullied and a religious duty is compounded with a wrongful act.

R. Isserlein is satisfied to a moral certainty that Gershom did intentionally injure Eliezer, the absence of legal proof notwithstanding. In such cases he argues that the court should impose punishment even though the strict Torah law does not require it. This is the same line of reasoning the Spanish masters used to justify their decisions in capital matters when there was governmental authority for their criminal jurisdiction. Here, however, there is no such governmental license. Nonetheless, when circumstances indicate that a special measure is called for in order to restore public order, this great Ashkenazic authority did not hesitate to impose one. The synagogue cannot be an arena for unpunishable battery.

R. Isserlein issues a "court order," so to speak, that Gershom should show remorse and seek pardon from his victim. He should go to synagogue when the Torah is read, and while it is on the reading lectern, he is to walk from his place to Eliezer's place, by way of the holy ark, and the leaders of the congregation are to go also. He is to declare to Eliezer that he, Gershom, has sinned against God and Eliezer. He is to specify the sin committed and beg pardon from God and Eliezer out of genuine remorse.

Gershom is to give Eliezer a reasonable sum set by R. Isserlein to cover the medical expenses incurred. He is also to give him two gold marks (?) which Eliezer, with the knowledge of two trustworthy gentlemen, is to give to the synagogue for support of whatever religious charity he may choose, since he receives the money as a fine, to strengthen this special measure for preservation of the public peace.

The fine was after all not collectable in Eliezer's day and age; it is part of a punitive process for Gershom. The medical cost is only a reasonable sum to cover actual amounts spent. No doubt because of the absence of clear proof of intent to injure, the expiation process does not appear to be either prolonged nor supplemented with a ban, flogging, or any other punitive element. There simply was no legal basis for them.

SUMMARY

Shulhan Arukh Hoshen Mishpat 1:1, 5, briefly states the modalities for mayhem and battery which a rabbinic court might invoke. Non-ordained judges may require the offender to pay both medical costs and lost wages for the victim; the gloss to the rule mentions that some judges who are of course not ordained nor resident in the Land of Israel will not assess even these amounts, but there is apparently no general practice to be overly careful in avoiding such assessments. Further, the court is to insist that the offender make his peace with the victim, and it may impose other fines as it sees fit. In paragraph five, the judges have the authority to place the offender under an excommunicatory ban until the offender shall have given the victim an amount of money which in the court's judgment is sufficient under the circumstances to cover costs and other items, whether or not the victim is satisfied with it. Communities are free to institute local measures, including fines, and other punitive measures, as the circumstances require; and these fines are collectable at all events.

In sum, the punitive modalities available to some Spanish communities included capital punishment and severe corporal punishment. In terms of Jewish law they were special measures that could be imposed on the authority of governmental license to do so. While these punishments are brutal, and even cruel, no rabbi ever raised the question of their morality. Two elements suggest a reason for this silence from men who were thoroughly aware of the ethical standards Jewish law strove to maintain. First, they possibly reflect a borrowing from non-Jewish practice. Such punishments had been — and still are — sanctioned under Moslem religious law in some parts of the world. Possibly the Jewish authorities felt they had to demonstrate to their neighbors that they could be as rigorous as anyone else when it came to matters of blasphemy or homicide. Second, Jewish legal tradition itself does not necessarily frown on severe punishment for clearly guilty offenders: the *Resh Galutha* had authorized blinding, R. Huna authorized amputation of the hand, and the four modes of execution of the classic law are quite brutal. Jewish tradition does not quail at severity of punishment merely because it is severe and even bloody. Even so, the crippled convict we met earlier, according to *Ritba*, was still a Jew and could not be abandoned by the community. They had to provide him with some means of livelihood.

When these capital and corporal modalities were not available to the court, the tenor of punition is entirely different. The emphasis becomes the restoration of peace and order. After all, the subject under notice here is modalities for the maintenance of public safety and order. The offender Simha was under a court order to embark upon a life-long program of special remembrance and good works after a period of public humiliation and repentance. He also had to assist his victim's survivors. In effect, he was to follow a plan that did restore peace and order. That was the ultimate goal of all the court ordered activity.

The modes of punition for mayhem and battery appear to have been applied in combination. The offender had to make some financial amends; pay medical costs and the like to the satisfaction of the court. Probably an excommunicatory ban against the offender was in place until he complied with the court order against him. He may have suffered a flogging, apparently the only available corporal penalty. If any local ordinances provided for special duties and obligations, including fines, the offender had to satisfy them.

One theme that runs through the material from the time of the Geonim and onward is the necessity to confront the victim and publicly seek both divine and human pardon for what had been done. The demand that the offender seek forgiveness and pardon is more than the voice of moral outrage and a call for restoration of peaceful relations between antagonists. It is also punishment of the most exquisite variety. The offender must publicly abandon all defenses and pretenses, admit to his wrongdoing and beg the pardon of God and his victim. He is alone and psychologically naked in his act. Whatever element of enlightened morality this demand may carry with it, and whatever measure of restorative justice it may bring to the community, it is for the offender a hard and lasting punishment, a disgrace that cannot be hidden and a personal memory that cannot be effaced. Such an event in a Jewish community must have been memorable, brought to mind year after year as an enduring caution to maintain public peace and order, lest one become subject to a similar court order. The person who stood up in public and followed the orders of the court acted with a high degree of moral courage because public humiliation is not easily nor willingly borne. The call for the parties to reconcile, whether that brought a true reconciliation or not, should not be considered a mere slap on the wrist for a serious offender. The person who undertook such a regimen, though once again a member in good standing of the community, doubtless forever bore the sense of shame and remorse he had been ordered to demonstrate before his friends and neighbors. Perhaps the lasting burden of such punishment is part of the reason we do not know what such court-ordered offenders actually did, and what became of them. Humiliation may be sufficient reason for a person to abandon the community, to move away, even to seek sanctuary in the church or the mosque. However that may be, we remain in the dark as to what the offenders did or did not do.

The punitive modalities for the maintenance of public safety and public order were powerful indeed. We turn our attention now to modalities that, in the main, attempt to curb and prevent acts that disturb the public peace and order rather than prescribe the punishment of offenders.

Preventive and Coercive Modalities

Medieval Jewish law presents a number of modalities that are, in varying degrees, intended to prevent disruptions of the public peace or to coerce persons suspected of such behavior to desist from it. The line between preventive measures and coercive measures is indistinct at times since one modality may clearly be more preventive and another basically coercive. The modalities may also appear at first to be thoroughly punitive, and clearly a punitive element is present in some of them. Their purpose, however, is ultimately to prevent matters from getting out of hand rather than simply to punish for past wrongdoing. Some of these modalities have clear talmudic bases. They all involve the execution of a court order, either from a rabbinic court or from the organ of communal government charged with the maintenance of the public peace, that is, *berurim, adelantados,* the "seven good men of the city" and so forth.

A Capital Penalty

Suppression of informers required the court to impose a capital penalty if at all possible. This penalty was deemed a special measure ordered by the appropriate Jewish court to prevent an informer from carrying out his intended purpose of giving information to non-Jewish authorities to the eventual harm of Jewish people or Jewish property. We have encountered the figure of the informer before; Saul was tarred with that brush and *Rivash's* responsa, as we shall presently see, concerned a person who was thought to be an informer but in his judgment was not.

The informer in medieval Jewish life was the object of contempt and horror. Whether he acted from some animus against his fellows or for the sake of power or profit accruing to him from his non-Jewish masters, he was the achilles heel of the peace and order of the Jewish community. His secret word could spread fear and terror in the community, disrupting the lives of many and sending shock waves to weaken the always precarious stability of Jewish life.

The talmudic basis for neutralizing the informer is rooted in the concept of the *rodef,* the pursuer. The *rodef* in the classic law, *m.Sanh.* 8:9, is the person who is actively pursuing a male victim in order to kill him or to sodomize him; or a female victim, who is a betrothed *na'arah,* in order to rape her. Persons who come upon the *rodef* in the process of pursuing (or subduing) the victim are permitted to stop the *rodef* by whatever means are necessary to do so, even by killing him if no lesser level of force will suffice to halt the crime in progress. Once the unlawful act has been performed, however, the permission to stop the pursuer by any means necessary no longer exists. He is no longer a pursuer. He is a criminal who is, in theory, subject to other provisions of the law which are supposed to lead to condign punishment.

This basis in the Talmud is amplified by two rabbinic stories in which the power of the concept of *rodef* clearly emerges. The stories are about incidents of informing. They are neither ethically uplifting nor inspiring, but they are part of the talmudic record that is after all the foundation for the medieval modalities we are examining.

The first incident, and by far the less convoluted one, appears in *b.B.Qam.* 117a. A man wanted to provide the government with information concerning another man's straw. Possibly the straw would be taxed or even confiscated. We are not told those facts. The would-be informer appeared before the Amora Rav (third-century Babylonia). Rav told him not to inform, but the man persisted, saying I shall indeed show the straw to officials of the government. R. Kahana, who was present there, thereupon tore out the would-be informer's windpipe, certainly a mortal injury. The situation prompted two responses by Rav. He first quoted Isa 51:20, "Your sons have fainted; they lie at the head of every street as a bull in a net," on which he commented that just as a bull caught in a net receives no mercy, so too when a Jew's property comes into non-Jewish hands no mercy is shown. Possibly the reference is that no mercy is shown to the owner of that property, or perhaps the reference is to the property. Rashi comments ad loc. that Rav is telling R. Kahana that he did well by dispatching the would-be informer. Rav's second response was to advise R. Kahana to decamp to Palestine since the Sassanian government would consider what he did as simply a culpable homicide. The implication is that the killing could not be defended before the government as a measure to prevent an outrage against the internal order of the Jewish community.

The second incident appears in *b.Ber.* 58a. In this rather complicated narrative, R. Shela (fourth-century Babylonia) had a Jew flogged for having had sexual intercourse with a non-Jewish woman. Apparently, when Jews exercised any legal jurisdiction within their own community, it did not extend to corporal punishment, at least not for this alleged offense. The man went to the government and complained, an act that would have been meaningless if Jews were allowed to impose corporal punishment. The man said that there was a person among the Jews who was rendering judgment (and imposing punishment!) without royal license to do so. The government took the complaint seriously. An official investigated the matter and asked the Rabbi why he had punished the man with lashes. R. Shela replied that the person had had sex with a she ass! He was asked to produce witnesses for this and the rabbi brought forward the prophet Elijah from the shades — in human form and no doubt in contemporary dress — who testified to the matter. Elements of both fact and fancy mix freely in this ancient story. The appearance of the prophet Elijah to support R. Shela demonstrates beyond cavil that Jewish tradition supported R. Shela in everything he did, no matter how questionable his actions may appear in modern eyes.[1] The government officials, satisfied with the demonstration, declared that the man was indeed guilty of a capital crime. R. Shela responded (no doubt with a sigh) that Jews no longer had capital jurisdiction and the government could deal with the man as they wished. While the government people were conferring, R. Shela waxed rhapsodic about the earthly royalty that God in his mercy had fashioned on the divine model, and that the government was a lover of justice. The government agents thereupon appointed R. Shela to judicial office, presenting him with the staff that signified his authority to impose punishment.

R. Shela's flogging victim was incensed at this turn of events, and asked the Rabbi if God worked miracles for liars. R. Shela, never at a loss for words, cited Ezek 23:20, "Their flesh is like the flesh of asses," thus apparently substantiating, as far as he was concerned, his assertion to the government officials that the man had had connection with an animal. R. Shela saw that the man was about to repair once more to the government and reveal the web of lies that the Rabbi had spun. He said, "The man is a *rodef.*" Thus we have the establishment of a clear connection of the informer as the pursuer. R. Shela also said, with Exod 22:1 in mind, that if someone comes to kill you, you kill them first. At that point, R. Shela hit the man with his staff of judicial office and killed him.

It is noteworthy that in Rav's case the potential informer was specifically told to refrain from giving his information. R. Shela's victim received no such warning. In Rav's case the potential informant died for what he intended to do; he had not yet committed the act. In R. Shela's case the informant had already gone to the government once. His second trip to inform would doubtless have carried very serious consequences for R. Shela. R. Shela killed him before he could give the report; again, he was killed for what he intended to do, not for what he had already done. Both the element of prior warning against informing and the extreme step taken to prevent an act not yet accomplished are significant in the formulation of the medieval modality to suppress the informer. The acts of R. Kahana and R. Shela were preventive measures indeed.

The talmudic modality for dealing with informers was a swift death. The medieval authorities in Spain translated the two incidents we have noted into what

---

1 Even modern critical scholarship appears to find nothing amiss with R. Shela's response to governmental inquiry into his judicial activities and the killing of the would-be informant. Prof. Neusner dismisses the reference to Elijah as in actuality, the probable timely arrival of someone who supported R. Shela's story of bestiality. But of course this "witness" testified to be a lie – no bestiality had in fact occurred – and the entire allegation rested on a patent insult to all non-Jews. Later authorities accepted the presence of Elijah without further comment. See, Jacob Neusner, *A History of the Jews in Babylonia 2: The Early Sasanian Period*, StPB 11 (1966) 32–34.

might be characterized as a standing court order to kill the informer, indeed to do that was a meritorious act. As in the talmudic precedents, no hearing or trial or qualified witnesses were necessary, only the known expressed intent to give information to non-Jewish authorities.

SPANISH COMMUNITIES

In the Spanish communities where Jews exercised capital jurisdiction under royal license, informing was a capital crime. This threat to the peace and order of the Jewish community could not be tolerated. Two responsa present a clear picture of the preventive modality designed for informers.

RASHBA

The first responsum is from *Rashba*. It is by way of a commentary on the cases of Rav and R. Shela.[2] The inquirer poses a question that from time to time doubtless had serious practical implications where Jewish communities exercised criminal jurisdiction. He is asked about the incident in *b.B.Qam.* 117a, and cites the passage including the verse from Isaiah suggesting that Jewish lives and property are shown no mercy once they fall under non-Jewish power. The specific question is "Should a person be put to death on the basis of a statement of intent to inform? Is there not still an element of doubt as to whether or not the actual informing will occur? How can a person be executed on the basis of a doubt? Perhaps it is merely a case of a boast that may not be carried out, as in the statement of R. Nahman (*b.Šebu.* 46b) who said that if a man held an axe and threatened to cut down his neighbor's tree, and the tree is later found felled, one does not assume that the boaster cut it down, an element of doubt as to culpability remains.

Rashba does not accept such an argument in the case of the informer at all. For him the informer is a poisonous snake and whoever steps forward to kill it has performed a meritorious act. As for the element of doubt in the matter, if the person is wont to act this way (that is, to inform) then the mere statement of intent is sufficient. The statement is taken as the completed act. The person is then like one who comes to kill whom you may kill in self defense, the position of R. Shela in the *Berakhot* case. R. Shela did not wait to see what the man would do; he dispatched him forthwith.

Rashba expands this point. Even if only property is involved in the information to be given, it is as if the informant "killed him." We do not wait until after he "kills" the victim to take action. Clearly *Rashba* is asserting a preventive modality.

2 *Responsa of R. Solomon b. Adret,* 1:181.

Further, writes *Rashba,* when it is clear that a person intends to inform, even though he is not wont to do so, we have the *Baba Qamma* case: the matter stands as if we had certain knowledge that the person would inform, and the person is to die even with (a lingering) doubt. Others may step forward to save the potential victim by killing the potential informer. Finally, *Rashba* forecloses the possibility of mercy completely: we do not entertain the idea that this pursuer and informant may repent and not carry out his expressed intent.

The questioner is thus informed that the court may use the extreme penalty to prevent the possibility of informing. The expressed intent is taken as the completed act, and the possibility of repentance is dismissed. The informer is a marked man. We have on the basis of this responsum a virtual standing order for the court, when it has the authority to impose such penalties, to execute the informer. Prevention of harm to the community comes foremost.

ROSH

The *Rosh* details the case of another informer. The responsum presents an actual situation and its resolution.[3] The text is therefore significant both as a local decision, which approves and applauds the death penalty for an informant, and as a glimpse into the life of a Jewish community faced with a dangerous and delicate situation.

The inquiry apparently issued from the community of Seville. The questioner sought guidance for dealing with a man concerning whom it had become public knowledge that he is an informer against specific individuals and the community. He continually threatens that he will go and speak to powerful and violent persons about individuals and communities. He speaks of the harm he would be able to cause them, both to their persons and their property. The community fears this man very much, because he is regularly in attendance at the court of one of the most powerful magnates; obviously the community is properly concerned for itself and for the individuals involved since the informer is a person well connected with non-Jewish power. But that is not the end of the problem, of course.

The Jews have secretly been given authorization by the Crown to try this person, and if he is convicted on a capital charge, to execute him. The informer is apparently unaware that he is in jeopardy. He might well be under the illusion that his position is secure because his non-Jewish masters would protect him from Jewish retribution. But informants play a dangerous game. Their presence might become an embarrassment to their masters. Their usefulness may decline. They may overplay their hand, as perhaps this one did through

3 *Responsa of R. Asher b. Yehiel,* 17:1.

his threats. The informant may not enjoy the security from harm that he supposes surrounds him.

In any event the inquiry has gone forward. The heads of the community have convened a court to investigate whether or not the aforementioned public knowledge about this person is correct. They take testimony, according to which they will decide what seems to be the proper course of action.

The substance of the testimony is then presented. R. and S. testified before the hearing court that it is clear to them that this man is an established informer. He has threatened Jews many times by supplying false information. (A true report would have been bad enough, of course.) False information opens every portal of danger and disaster. For a month past, while Don Pedro has been in Seville, and this man was making his threats, one of the community leaders entreated him to stop his threats but he would not desist from his calumnies. R. and S. also testified that in their opinion the leaders among the elders of the community and the men of the community feared that he would go and lie about the community. Others also testified that he was an established informer, and that he had uttered threats in their presence many times.

The questioner then addressed *Rosh*: Shall this person be judged as a *rodef* since he proceeds to lie while Don Pedro is here, and did not desist in spite of reproofs? May he be executed on the basis of R. Kahana's precedent — even though in this sort of case the Crown has authorized a death penalty upon conviction?

Rosh begins his response with the remark that since the ancient Sanhedrin went into exile, the four classic modes of execution have also fallen into desuetude. That is, says *Rosh*, a person is no longer convicted for the classic capital offenses: since there is no Sanhedrin, no Jewish court has the power to convict a person of them after the classic procedure. Yet, he continues, those persons whom we kill, as specified in *b.Sanh.* 73a, that is, save from sinning by taking their lives, are not killed for something they have done, but for something they propose to do — to save the pursued from death or evil occurrences (rape). These prosecutions have not fallen into desuetude provided that royal license authorizes the Jewish court to adjudicate such cases. *Rosh* argues that those latter cases do not depend on the classic elements of a capital trial before the Sanhedrin, but rather upon what any man can readily see with his own eyes under the principle enunciated in the verse "You shall not stand idly by the blood of your neighbor..." (Lev 19:16). The *rodef* who would inform against his fellow's property is equated to the informer against his person. Once the person has been taken into the power of violent people because of information against him, no mercy is shown him. Today they take a little of his property, tomorrow, all of it, finally they threaten to kill him — perhaps he will confess he has more property somewhere! Thus the informer against property is a pursuer who may be stopped from committing his crime by the sacrifice of his life.

Rosh then recapitulates part of the question: witnesses testify that while Don Pedro was there in town, this man threatened to inform and one of the Jewish leaders pleaded with him to stop, but he would not. In *Rosh's* opinion this is precisely the situation that R. Kahana faced.

Here in this case as well, once the Jewish leader had pleaded with him to stop, and he had refused, his life was fair game, at least in theory, for any Jew to take. *Rosh* then echoes *Rashba's* sentiment: whoever steps forward to kill him has acted meritoriously. He continues by asserting that if they had ordered a non-Jewish assassin to kill him then indeed they had done well, because even if it were not at the precise time of the commission of the offense of informing, we learn in *b.ʾAbod. Zara* 26 a–b that "we bring informers down." This is interpreted as meaning that the informer is thrown in a pit from which he cannot escape and would therefore, in time, die. We do not actually lay murderous hands on him following the view of the Amora R. Abbahu. The order to the non-Jewish assassin to kill the man is tantamount to throwing him in the pit, which involves physical touching of the offender by the person or persons executing the order. *Rosh* then cites an anonymous responsum to the effect that it is permissible to engage a gentile assassin to kill him even though the offender is not engaged in the actual commission of the offense, as a *rodef* in the Talmud is.

Rosh does add that there is an opinion that prohibits the employment of a non-Jewish assassin to deal with the informer when he is not actually committing the offense. He cites an argument of his teacher (R. Meir of Rothenburg) that dismisses such an argument. We are not, however, to be swayed from engaging the assassin on the mere possibility that the informer repented of his wrongdoing in his heart and had thereby purged himself of culpability. The responsum emphasizes that according to the testimony the man has threatened, he has been warned to desist, and thus may be deemed "in actual commission of the offense." Everyone is authorized to kill him.

It is furthermore, according to the *Rosh*, unnecessary to take testimony in his presence. This procedural element is also found in *Rivash's* review of procedure in capital cases which we have already noticed. The reason that testimony may be taken in his absence is the possibility which we have noted that the established informant will be protected by his non-Jewish masters. Thus if it were necessary to conduct the trial in his presence, no case could ever be successfully prosecuted. If the informer spreads his lies against individuals and groups even when he is not in danger, how much the more would he put Jews in peril when he is in mortal danger himself. As we have noted, however, in this case the Crown has already authorized trial and execution upon conviction. The informer, it seems, was not always secure against punishment though doubtless many an informer did rely on powerful connections to rescue him when a community had resolved to put every man's hand against him.

Rosh concludes his responsum with some guidance. He declares the practice of Jewish communities has become that when an informer has on three occasions betrayed either property or persons to non-Jewish authorities, the community seeks counsel and guidance to remove this informer from the world as a special preventive measure. Others will be chastened by this example and informers will not increase. Therefore in this case, where witnesses have testified that a man was an established informer, and also that he was in active commission of the offense, they have done well to sentence him to be hanged.

We do not have any idea what happened to the informer. Perhaps the sentence of the court was carried out, perhaps not. What we do know is that when the Jewish community had the authority to execute offenders, the informer was surely a marked man. The preventive modality was death. There is never a hint of mercy or clemency. When a person chose to play the informer's game, he stepped across an invisible line that effectively separated him from the more humane elements of Jewish tradition. The informer was of course held liable for making good any financial losses he may have caused other Jews through his informing activities. But those matters fall outside the area of modalities for the maintenance of public peace and public order.

SHULHAN ARUKH HOSHEN MISHPAT RESTATEMENT

The *Shulhan Arukh Hoshen Mishpat* 388:9, 10 and 11 summarize the preventive modalities pertaining to the informer. The gloss to 388:9 states that one may save himself from an informer by turning him in (to the community leaders?) provided that the informer had already on a previous occasion informed against the victim. Paragraph ten restates the matter in detail. It is permissible to kill anyone at any place if that person has informed the non-Jewish government with respect to a fellow Jew's person or property. This holds good even at the present time when the death penalties of the classic law no longer obtain. The potential informer is to be warned against committing such an offense if it is at all possible to tender such a warning. If the person remains obdurate, it is then a religious duty to kill him. Paragraph eleven simply states that once the act of informing has occurred, it is no longer permissible to kill the informer unless the person has established a reputation of repeated offenses of this kind. In that case the informer may be killed to prevent him from harming others. Clearly the law presents a preventive modality; the informer is to be stopped, even before he commits the offense, when his status as an informer is well-known.

When a community did not have governmental authority to pursue informers, a death penalty was certainly not an option, though possibly a mysterious assassination was not out of the realm of possibility given the utter horror Jewish communities felt for the informer. Other possible modalities were the excommunicatory ban, of which more later, and no doubt flogging. But the communities had to proceed with caution at all times. The non-Jewish authorities might spirit the informer away from their grasp. In any event, public peace and order could not endure unless the atmosphere of fear and uncertainty an informer caused could be dispelled. The community employed a preventive modality — death, the sure prophylactic against the known, or suspected, informer.

UNWANTED SEXUAL ADVANCES

Informing was not the only potential threat to public order that called for a preventive measure. Unwanted sexual advances also had the potential to cause serious disruption in community life. Medieval Jewish law adapted several modalities to curb just such a potential threat. One such modality amounts to "injunctive relief." We are, it must be clear, not concerned here with provable improper acts. We are looking at suspicion, at something that might or might not reflect the reality of some unlawful behavior. The key is prevention; the community may take steps to see that suspicion does not blossom into a disruptive reality. The matter appears in a responsum of *Rivash*.[4]

Rivash reviewed an inquiry from the *Beruré Averot* of Algeciras. Algohar, the wife of Jacob b. Joseph, raised a complaint about Isaac Cohen, that he comes upon her unawares and says to her that he loves her. He kept on in this fashion until he said ". . . Give me a kiss so that I won't die because of love for you!" On another occasion, he called her to come to his house. He paraphrased Prov 27:16, "A continual dripping on a rainy day, and a contentious woman are alike . . ." He cited the first part of the verse, saying, "There is a continual dripping in the house," which may have meant that all was not well between him and his wife. This may have been some sort of slang or perhaps a more elegant rephrasing of an improper advance. At any rate, she understood his statement to be a wicked suggestion. She alleges that he said lewd things to her, and that he is accustomed to do this to other women!

Isaac Cohen responded to the woman's statements and denied ever having harbored any evil intent. Heaven forbid! Because they were neighbors, he contended, they engaged in joking banter as lovers might do. He asserts that he would never make a general practice of doing this because he is a Jew who enjoys an unimpeachable family reputation.

The *berurim* inquired of the woman why she had not raised this complaint about him before because of the numerous times, according to her, that Isaac

4 *Responsa of R. Isaac b. Sheshet*, no. 265.

had followed her. She responded that she was afraid that her husband would get into an argument with him and they would try to kill each other. Here we have, of course, the threat to public order. The misbehavior of the one man could easily lead to mortal combat and to others siding with one party or the other, thus public peace and order would suffer.

The *berurim* also asked her if she had any witnesses to the unwanted advances. She mentioned the name of one man, to whom she had confided her story. He, however, testified upon his oath that he had no independent knowledge of anything she had said. He only knew what she had told him. He had asked her why she had not made an official complaint before, and she answered that she did not want her husband to have a quarrel with any Jew.

The woman further said before the *berurim* that they had already issued a warning that Isaac should not speak with the wife of Samuel Peniel nor to go with her to any place that might raise suspicion of unlawful behavior. R. Isaac responded that the warning had been due to a quarrel he had had with Peniel six years earlier. There had been no breath of suspicion from that quarter ever since.

What we have in these complaints and answers is a matter of unwanted advances. The problem is that those advances could lead to a serious disruption of the peace, but nothing has happened yet, and we have only claim and counter claim in any event. There is nothing that could properly be called an offense in any real sense. How then can this behavior, if true, be prevented from eventually causing harm?

Rivash's first comment clears the air. Since the woman has no witnesses against Isaac, it is not proper to accept her unsupported word, nor to suspect him in this unseemly matter nor to impose penalty or punishment upon him on the basis of her statements. At this point *Rivash* introduces the modality of separation, a sort of "injunction," commanding Isaac, under pain of an excommunicatory ban, to refrain from speaking with the woman on any matter. This will separate them from the possibility of unlawful behavior with each other. Similarly they are not to dwell in the same immediate neighborhood. Although he does not specify which one should move away, one rather presumes it is the man who must find other quarters.

Rivash then addresses the *berurim* directly: if the man is indeed suspect in matters of sexual impropriety, even though there are no witnesses to such matters that would raise them to the status of an actual offense, it is fitting to rebuke the man with a seven-day excommunication and straightly warn him in dire terms that if he does not comport himself properly that he would be cast out of the community and pushed away with two hands. This clearly implies the modality of excommunication as a preventive measure, and even the modality of exile from the community. He supports this modality by a reference to classic law that speaks of flogging, *b.Qidd.* 81a: a person may be flogged because of evil rumors that circulate about him. Clearly there is nothing substantial by way of accusation, only persistent rumors.

The rule is based on the amoraic reading of 1 Sam 2:24, where Eli is understood to assert a negative injunction, a "thou shalt not," with regard to negative reports, thus allowing the infliction of a rabbinical flogging on one who transgresses that negative injunction and concerning whom an evil rumor has spread. Rivash also cites the text of this rule as it appears in the Maimonidean restatement of the *halakhah, Hilkhoth Sanhedrin* 24:5, a chapter that specifies various penalties available to the Jewish court. Maimonides holds that the court may flog a person who is the subject of evil rumors concerning his sexual morality, provided that the rumor is persistent and the person has no known enemies who would spread such a rumor.

The talmudic text does not mention the ban or for that matter the injunction. The court presumably may take these steps because it *is* the court and it possesses powers to impose various types of punishment or, as in this case, to take steps to prevent the suspected behavior from becoming a reality.

Thus, the "injunction" really has no specific talmudic basis, but the flogging and the excommunication – with the threat of exile – are all part of the talmudic matrix from which medieval Jewish law developed this modality for preserving public order. There is the preventive modality of separation, and the modalities of excommunication, flogging, and exile are invoked to prevent even the suspicion of unlawful behavior from raising problems in the community. The modalities are certainly preventive and manifestly coercive as well. In fine, people may be coerced to conduct themselves in such a manner that not even a rumor about them may gain any credence. The line between preventive and coercive modalities is at times too thin to make any significant practical difference. Prevention and coercion stand together.

Excommunicatory Ban

From time to time, the excommunicatory ban has been mentioned. This is perhaps the best known of the medieval modalities for the maintenance of public peace and order, and it rests upon well established talmudic, and even biblical, foundations. The threat of the ban acts as a preventive: one would not do such and such an act because to do so involves the risk of excommunication. If, however, one does the proscribed act, the power of the ban is clearly coercive, exerting a force on the person in order to bring him (or her) back to the Jewish fold as a full member once again. Indeed there is also a punitive element to it, but the ban may be lifted and the person restored to the community; that is the preferred outcome when an excommunication is involved. The ban serves two purposes in this review: it is preventive and if necessary coercive.

The possibility of doing something deserving of a full and open-ended excommunication in the rather small and tightly knit medieval Jewish communities, where one-thousand souls would have been a large group indeed, posed a serious problem for the individual Jew. To run afoul of the law and incur communal wrath to the extent of such an excommunication meant separation from virtually everything that gave the individual's life meaning and dimension. He was cut off from the majority of his fellow Jews; and though the doors of the church or the mosque were ever open, that was a desperate step indeed. The person would then be forever severed from his or her Jewish past, present and future.

The tradition tells us in clear language how the excommunicant was to be treated by Jews, but there is no word on how the non-Jewish community might react to the person. Would he or she be treated with derision and contempt? Would he or she be hounded to convert? Would he or she be greeted as a brave and independent spirit by non-Jews? There were indeed deep and treacherous waters for the excommunicant to navigate. Perhaps far better was to yield to the coercive force of the ban and rejoin the Jewish community. These medieval excommunicants were not diarists whose daily comments and reactions would have provided invaluable insight into the recesses of their world. The fact that in the course of time excommunication lost much of its force, as winds of change came to Jewish communities and eventually emancipation altered their complexion entirely, does not however reflect the reality of the period here under notice.

As for the preventive element of the ban, there is no way to prove a negative. That is, there is no way to determine how many people refrained from breaking the law because the threat of the ban acted as a preventive measure. An excommunication in one form or another could be appended to any local ordinance so that an offender could be placed under a ban forthwith. Perhaps that clause did prevent a good many from treating laws cavalierly. For instance, the famous *herem* of Rabbenu Gershom (tenth-century Rhineland) that, among other things, outlawed polygamy, may well have been a significant element in discouraging polygamy; in any event, monogamy had already been the standard Jewish marital configuration for over one thousand years (with only a few well known exceptions, for example, the Jews of Yemen until the mid twentieth century). The threat of the ban certainly served some preventive function over the centuries.

The form of the ban that appears most often in the materials on maintenance of peace and order is the *niddui,* or as it is also known, the *shamta.* This type of ban is traced to the biblical order of Ezra (10:8); in that biblical exemplar the offender faced both confiscation of property and personal excommunication. The mildest form of the ban was the *nezifah,* a public rebuke which required the person rebuked to retire to his home and stay there for seven days. In Babylonia the confinement was for one day (see *b.Mo^ced Qat.* 16a).

The more severe *shamta* (often simply called the *niddui*) was in effect a type of curse. It was both a criminal punishment and a coercive modality. Its usefulness as a preventive measure is more to the point here; its purpose was obviously not purely punitive since a *niddui* ban could be lifted once the person had seen the error of his ways and made appropriate amends. The *shamta*, which was pronounced by a rabbinic court, was imposed for thirty days during which a person was effectively removed from much of the life of the Jewish community, though by no means all of it: he could enjoy the company of immediate family, teach and learn, and engage in business. The court pronouncing the *niddui* was at liberty to impose lighter or stricter requirements upon the person. For instance, the person under the ban had to eschew laundered clothing and having his hair cut; he might in some situations have his ritual fringes cut off and suffer even more public embarrassment. The *shamta-niddui* might be extended for an additional thirty days. If the person was still recalcitrant after sixty days of such conditions, a full and open-ended excommunication could be solemnly pronounced. A person under the full excommunicatory ban was for all intents and purposes Jewishly dead; he was in *herem* which continued even post-mortem in terms of funerary practices. This type of open-ended ban even affected the family of the excommunicant, since it had to bear the public shame of its excommunicated member. It is reasonable to suppose that only the most recalcitrant and unyielding offenders would need more than sixty days of such separation from the community. One was therefore under severe coercion to acknowledge his wrongdoing, make amends, and seek pardon and return to normal status.

The medieval authorities could and did attach a penalty of excommunication for persons who offended against their local ordinances and certainly this civil modality was applied to people who offended against Torah law. The number of cases involving *niddui* (and *herem*) is enormous. Not all of them involved public order, but offenses that did could be handled by a *niddui* whose purpose was not only punitive, but coercive (and indeed preventive) to bring the person back into the fold and keep others from his folly.

Rashba notes that all punishments (presumably including *niddui* and *herem*) should be used sparingly as special measures made necessary by the need of the time.[5] The *Rosh* echoes this sentiment of his contemporary and asserts a rather definitive policy statement for the guidance of all communities in these matters of the excommunicatory ban and all other forms of coercive and preventive measures (and indeed in purely punitive measures as well).[6] *Rosh* asserts

---

5 Baer, *History of the Jews*, 1:284.
6 *Responsa of R. Asher b. Yehiel*, 6:27.

that a community may take whatever steps are necessary, as the need of the hour demands, to erect a protective barrier around the Torah. If the offender is a poor man and economic measures will not be effective with him, he may be punished with flogging, and incarceration; he bases this opinion on *b.Mo*ᶜ*ed Qat.* 16a that details what an offender may expect to face by way of punishment and coercion. *Rosh* is quite willing to see a recalcitrant person exposed to all manner of exemplary punishment for not obeying ordinances, and so on; and he even advises the use of non-Jewish agents to force the Jew to obey. One concludes from the opinion of *Rosh* (and *Rashba*) that coercion should be applied only when necessary and reasonable, but when circumstances indicate that it is appropriate, the full arsenal may be turned against the offender, including excommunication.

The excommunicatory ban, in any of its forms, clearly served as a threat and thus a form of prevention and as a coercive modality to impress the offender with the error of his ways and force him to return in humility to a more righteous life. It is clearly a modality with great flexibility. It does more than merely prevent, or purely punish, because it warns off potential evildoers who can anticipate its force on the one hand, and presses actual evildoers to repent and return to piety. This ban was often simply a clause in, for example, a communal ordinance. The penitent who returns to the community after the ban has been lifted has not been rehabilitated in any modern sense. There is no monitored period of treatment or training that he or she must face. The person has simply undertaken to live free of previous wrongdoing and has accepted his punishment, including public abasement, for past misdeeds. He or she is perfectly well aware of what is expected of him or her and rejoins the community duly chastened. Any "rehabilitation," so to speak, is the person's own resolve to do the right.

INTIMIDATION

We turn now to the final modality in this section on preventive (and coercive) measures to maintain public peace and order. This next measure has clear talmudic roots and a striking medieval application. Rabbi Shimon b. Zemah Duran (the *Rashbatz*, Majorca and North Africa, late fourteenth century) demonstrates a purely coercive modality employed in the interests of justice and clearly for the purpose of maintaining peace and order in the community. The modality which is adapted from a talmudic procedure is simply coercive: threat and intimidation to extract a confession when there is no actual evidence to prove the case against the accused. In the Talmud, coercion through the use of force (the stocks) wrung confessions from suspected forgers (*b.B.Bat.* 167b). In a case of theft, Mar Zutra saw a rabbinical student wash his hands and then dry them on someone else's clothing. Thereupon he ordered the man to be seized and put in stocks with the assertion that he was the guilty party because he showed no concern for another's property. The man confessed to the theft (b.B.Meṣ. 24a).

Mar Zutra's approach to the matter might appear to be capricious and perhaps unsound. Actually what he did was quite sound and indeed it is perhaps
the first documented use in criminal investigation of a very modern investigative tool: behavioral profiling.[7] The theory is that a person's basic behavioral
pattern will appear in some form in whatever the person undertakes to do.
Thus one might reasonably project that a person who has no respect for other's
property may very well be involved in theft. The reasonable projection turned
out to be accurate: he confessed. The Talmud does not raise the age old chal-
lenge to such a confession – such a statement given under duress is of very
questionable value.

Rashbatz also faced a case of theft in which there was no good evidence
against the accused.[8] R., a blind man, traveled in the company of S. R. had some
pearls sewn into clothing. S. and R. kept close company on the journey and slept
near each other. When R. looked for the pearls, he did not find them. He suspected S. of stealing them since S. was a person of bad reputation. S. denied the
accusation. Rashbatz was asked what should be done.

Rashbatz begins his responsum with a classic statement that would evoke
the agreement of peace officers the world over. He says that it is well known
that the thief does not practice his thievery where there are witnesses who can
see and identify him. The obvious is sometimes worth reiteration. Therefore
he says that if the court were limited in its work by having to decide cases only
where there were witnesses, justice would be severely disadvantaged. He then
echoes what we have seen his predecessors assert, that every judge in every
generation has the authority to take special measures to make certain that justice is not badly served.

He then mentions the talmudic precedents already reviewed in this essay
that support his view. The court imposes flogging and other penalties that are
not in accordance with the law, as a means of protecting the system of Jewish
law as a whole (b. Yebam. 90b). How much more, writes the respondent, is such
a measure proper in order to rescue a victim from his oppressor and a poor
wretch from his tormentor. Rashbatz here introduces the talmudic anecdote
about Mar Zutra.

He follows the statement of Mar Zutra's investigative coup with the declaration that in the case before him, it seems both reasonable and plausible that S.
is a thief. The victim is blind (and cannot offer any reliable information about
what he actually might have seen!). The author cites a sort of biblical parallel

7 Stephen M. Passamaneck, "Ancient Traces of Investigative Profiling," Jewish Law Association Studies 10 (2000) 141–48.

8 Shimon B. Zemah Duran, Responsa of R. Shimon b. Zemah Duran (ed. Amsterdam, 1738–39) vol. 3
no. 168.

to the case of this blind man, 2 Chr 20:35–37. In the biblical passage Jehosophat, King of Judah, allied himself with the wicked King Aháziah. The two jointly built a fleet to attack Tarshish. Eliezer prophesied about Jehosophat that because he had allied himself with the wicked Aháziah God would destroy Jehosophat's works. The fleet was indeed lost. What happened in the case under notice, so to speak, was that S. put R. in a "place of bears and lions" and he "entered the city": that is, R. was ever in a vulnerable position just as Jehosophat had put himself in a vulnerable position. And so *Rashbatz* declares that the law allows us to intimidate S., to threaten to do thus and thus to him if he does not confess to the theft. Plainly threats, indeed dire threats, may be hurled against S. in order to extract a confession from him. He also cites *Tur Hoshen Mishpat* 64, where a responsum of *Rosh* is cited to the same effect. So far it appears that verbal intimidation is as far as matters might go, but Rashbatz adds an ominous note to what he has written.

He writes with obvious pride and satisfaction that he imprisoned a Jew who had been accused of thievery. He had put him in prison on the basis of the talmudic principle that words which are absolutely true are recognized as the truth. For example, Delilah knew that Samson was at last not telling her a lie; true words are recognizable as such (Judg 16:18). There was no official to release that Jew from prison. Afterward, says *Rashbatz*, the stolen property was found among his effects. The entire community had praised him for his diligence in the matter. Although incarceration is not mentioned with respect to S., certainly the threat of close confinement, or the stocks or perhaps a flogging were all possible threats. Imprisonment may have well been a next step on the road to a confession. While there is no need to envision the rack and the thumb screw, the Talmud clearly allows a level of physical intimidation as well as verbal intimidation to extract the confession. Confinement in stocks (or prison?) led to the confession of forgers in talmudic cases (*b.B.Bat.* 167a). Once the confession has been achieved, presumably there is no turning back or recanting for the accused. Threats and some level of physical force were perfectly legitimate coercive modalities in the service of public order and the peace of the community.

Preventive and coercive modalities have been taken as a single unit because the coercive power of a modality, for example, the ban, may well prevent an offender from reengaging in unlawful activity. By the same token a preventive measure, for example, separating parties by a sort of injunction, or a flogging, obviously represents a strong degree of coercion. The line between them is not distinct nor need it be. The only preventive modality that is at the same time entirely coercive is the death penalty for the informer; where that penalty was not an option, the coercive modality of the ban, or perhaps a flogging, was probably the most effective way of dealing with the problem. A preventive (or coercive) modality could be instituted on the basis of a reasonable suspicion of improper activity as *Rivash*'s responsum testifies. *Rashbatz*'s responsum demonstrates this ever more clearly: the wrongdoer was prevented from further activity and co-erced by close confinement until a confession was forthcoming.

In modern parlance, what *Rashbatz* did was nothing more than something akin to a reasonable cause arrest. There was at least reasonable cause to support the accusation of robbery. The further element, the truly coercive element, is that he appears to be prepared to keep the accused incarcerated until the mat-ter is resolved by his confession. To characterize Mar Zutra's act as a reasonable cause arrest is far more dubious; he acted on the strength of a "behavioral profile" and that falls well below the circumstances necessary for reasonable cause ar-rest, a term familiar in modern law enforcement: there was reasonable cause to hold the blind man's traveling companion.

One may of course quarrel with the morality of such approaches, but the rab-binical court clearly saw itself as the guardian of the public weal, and the obser-vance of proper Torah prescribed behavior as they understood it. Any threat to its sense of public order and public peace required stern measures. Once a person was suspected of crossing the line of acceptable behavior, the apparent rabbinic reliance on a concept of the greatest good for the greatest number pre-vailed. If this meant incarceration, flogging, or excommunicatory ban, or the necessity of changing one's residence, those were simply the approved conse-quences of the court's exercise of its proper powers. The medieval Jewish com-munity understood well the purposes and the means of prevention and coer-cion in matters of public order.

Protective Modalities

In this section we look at the steps that medieval Jews took, or might have initiated, to thwart an external threat to its peace and welfare. The Jews of the Middle Ages were not in a position to ward off external threats if they rose to the level of armed attack by Jew-hating mobs or armies supported actively or passively by local non-Jewish authorities. We shall look at one such occasion of mob violence presently. The external threats envisioned therefore include only the criminal behavior of a single Jew that would endanger the community; and the danger of fire.

External Threats

Protective modalities as the phrase is used here imply external threats of whatever origin. One such modality is the converse of the case of the informer. The informer was an internal threat, that could expose the community to dangers from the outside. No punishment was too severe for the informer, or even for the potential informer under the proper circumstances. The converse, however, does not hold true. The community retained the power to surrender one of its own when that person engaged in criminal acts that would occasion general harm when the host community forbade those acts, such as forgery, fraud and counterfeiting, and that person would not heed the remonstrances of the community to desist. This, to be sure, was more than a threat, but a serious reality: the person was a manifest lawbreaker. The community may deliver such a person to non-Jewish authority with the assurance that he alone is engaged in such criminal activity. No doubt such a step was taken only after the most profound soul searching on the part of the rabbinical court or the communal leadership. The non-Jewish authorities were not inclined to treat lawbreakers of this sort gently. Then, too, the counterfeiter might have information on others in the Jewish community that he could use as leverage to get the case against him reduced or even dropped. We are, after all, dealing with criminals, and this is exactly what criminals do or try to do. So the community's decision to turn the person in can never be without dangers, to the person of course, and quite possibly to others. But the protective modality of surrender is on the books; the greatest good for the greatest number appears to be the guiding principle (see *Shulhan Arukh Hoshen Mishpat* 388:12, gloss).

Perception

The major protective modality is not so much a modality in terms of a specific legal step or other overt action, but rather a matter of a slow change of perception concerning the implication of the law with respect to the external danger of fire with respect to violation of Sabbath rest.[1]

FIRST STAGE OF THE LAW

The first stage of the law concerning fighting a fire on the Sabbath explicitly prohibits it unless a life is mortally threatened by the blaze. If property is also saved as well as life, no violation of the Sabbath has occurred. In any event, putting out a fire for the purpose of saving property alone is forbidden. This rule however raises a difficulty. Saving life and saving property are not too easily separable in practice. The fire that at first threatens only property will soon be a threat to life if it rages unchecked. The *mishnah* acknowledges this important fact when it characterizes fire as mobile, and that characteristic puts it in a category of destructive causes all its own (*m.B.Qam.* 1:1). Further, fire, by its very nature, remains a danger unless extinguished, and that holds good for every day of the week. Therefore, if the law precludes Jews from fighting, and extinguishing, fire on the Sabbath in order to save property when no lives are in immediate danger, those Jews will soon face a more serious blaze that *does* endanger lives. Given that most Jews have been town or city dwellers over the last millennium and that fires were not an unusual danger in such places, a rigorous application of the law against Sabbath firefighting when only property is at risk will obviously put Jews at serious risk to life as well before very long. This risk appears to run counter to the rabbinic concept that the commandments are given to foster life and not to expose people to mortal danger.

Mishnah Šabbat, chapter sixteen, discusses the amounts and types of goods that one may rescue from a Sabbath fire and the mode of such rescue. The chapter begins with a permission to save holy Scriptures from fire and proceeds to specify amounts of food and clothing that may be rescued. *Mishnah* 8 allows for the setting of a fire break wall using containers, even if the containers are full of water which will break because of the heat and spill the water, which extinguishes the fire. *Mishnah* 9 directly addresses the matter of fire fighting: if a non-Jew comes to put the fire out, one neither encourages nor discourages him to do so, since Jews are not responsible for a non-Jew's observance of the Sabbath.

Further, *mishnah* 9 provides that if a Jewish boy, less than thirteen years of age, comes to put the fire out, Jews do *not* allow him to do so, since they are responsible for the boy's observance of the Sabbath. The *gemara* on this *mishnah*

---

1   A fuller treatment of this subject appears in the on-line journal *Melilah* published by the Manchester University Centre for Jewish Studies: http://www.mucjs.org/MELILAH/2005/2.pdf. I am grateful to the editors of *Melilah* who have granted me permission to reproduce much of the material published there.

(*b.Šabb.* 121a) introduces a statement by the *amora*, R. Ammi, to the effect that, regarding a fire occurring on the Sabbath, the Rabbis allowed one to declare, in the hearing of a non-Jew, "Anyone who extinguishes the fire is at no disadvantage." This statement obviously has to be directed toward a non-Jew since a Jew who puts out a fire on the Sabbath is indeed at a disadvantage: he has sinned grievously. This utterance is at odds with the strict neutrality of the mishnaic rule: neither encouragement nor discouragement may be offered. The codificatory material restates the rule: if a non-Jew comes to extinguish the fire, it is not necessary to discourage him. Over time R. Ammi's statement became part of the law, and was amplified to allow one to summon a non-Jew to the fire scene even though it is certain he will put the fire out when he arrives.

Three talmudic passages that present both the provision that requires strict neutrality toward a non-Jew who may put out a fire — neither encouraging not discouraging — and the provision that in effect allows encouragement to be given (*one is not at a disadvantage!*) introduce an anecdote, which appeared first in the *t.Šabb.* 13:9 and is repeated in all three of the talmudic citations (*b.Šabb.* 121a, *y.Šabb.* 16:15d and *y.Ned.* 4:38d). This anecdote illustrates the first of the four stages in the law about fighting fire on the Sabbath. It indicates an absolute refusal to fight fire on (or have non-Jews fight it on) the Sabbath unless of course human life is in danger. This refusal is the starting point for the slow changes that occurred.[2]

The talmudic material is adapted from the tosefta and cited as a *baraita*. The story goes that a fire once occurred in the courtyard of one Joseph b. Simai in the town of Shihin. The Roman troops garrisoned at Sepphoris (Shihin was visible from Sepphoris) came rushing to extinguish it, because Joseph b. Simai was a royal officer. He did not allow them to do so, because of the honor of the Sabbath. A miracle occurred. Rain fell and put out the fire. In the evening (when the Sabbath had ended) he sent two *sela*'s to each man and 50 *dinar* (*dinar* = 25 *shekel*s = 12½ *sela*'s) to their officer! When the Sages heard of this, they declared that it had not been necessary (to prevent the Roman troops from putting out the fire), because we have learned that when a non-Jew comes to put out a fire on the Sabbath, we neither encourage nor discourage him. The Sages had to be referring to his refusal to let the Romans fight the fire, because the justification for their view is the mishnaic statement that one need not encourage nor discourage the non-Jew who comes to fight the fire and Joseph b. Simai chose to discourage them. Perhaps from an excess of piety?

The tosefta version is less detailed: Joseph did not allow the men from the camp to extinguish the fire. Rain fell and extinguished the fire. The Sages said

---

2 The shift occurred over a period of 700 years more or less. The circumstances of Jewish life had altered many times in that period but the danger of fire was always present.

no compensation was necessary, nevertheless he sent a *sela'* to each man and 50 *dinar* to the officer. The Palestinian Talmud versions have Joseph telling the troops not to put out the fire saying, "let the collector collect his debt." This is doubtless an allusion to a divine act; God was collecting his due from Joseph. Again the story relates that he sent each man two *sela'*s and the officer 50 *dinar* when the Sabbath had ended. There is no mention of the Sages' opinion that he did not have to stop the Romans from fighting the fire. Fire fighting was moot anyway, since apparently divine intervention took care of the blaze.

All versions of the story make one clear point: Sages are quite content to have non-Jews do whatever they wish to do, but the Jew does not fight the fire on the Sabbath unless lives are in danger, an emphasis strongly made in the Palestinian Talmud material. The version in the Palestinian Talmud, *y.Šabb.* 16:15d and *y.Ned.* 4:38d, give additional detail. It seems that in R. Ammi's time a fire occurred in the village of Aphik (on a Sabbath of course). R. Ammi announced in the market place of the non-Jews, asserting that, whoever works (to put out the fire) is not at a disadvantage. Rabbi Elazar said before Rabbi Jose, "[It] was [a case of] danger [to life]. [The rejoinder]: if it was a case of danger to human life even R. Ammi should help put it out! Wherever there is danger to human life, one does not say, 'let the matter be done by women and children'" (the *Nedarim* version has "non-Jew").

Clearly, the duty to fight fire becomes the duty of everyone when life is in danger, and thus, as has been suggested, implicitly a duty of any given community of individuals since one person with a bucket or a blanket is no match for a roaring fire that poses mortal danger. There is, however, no discussion of what that "mortal danger" might be — is it from the fire, or from something else related to the fire?

The tosefta and the *baraitot* parallel to it present some intriguing possibilities if we reflect on the fact that in Joseph b. Simai's time a Roman fire fighting corps, a para-military unit, was a well-established institution in Rome. Further, Joseph b. Simai has been identified as an official in the service of Agrippa II who was a puppet "monarch" under the Romans in the mid-first century C.E., well before the revolt of 66. The Roman Emperor Claudius awarded him the office of Supervisor of the Jerusalem Temple. Although he took the title of king, he was never actually a king of Judea. Part of the Galilee was under his control, however, and Sepphoris was the capital of Galilee. It was also the site of a Roman military base.

The town of Shihin had a pottery industry, and it was claimed that a fire that started among the kilns was visible from Sepphoris. There is certainly no reason to identify the fire in Joseph b. Simai's "courtyard" with the fire at the kilns, but it is possible that in the course of time — our texts were all committed to writing long after the mid-first century C.E. — the fire in the kiln and the fire in the courtyard might have become recollected as a single event. Whatever the case may be, Joseph b. Simai, with his connection to the seats of power, was just the sort of personage whom the Romans would have aided. It is doubtful that the Romans would have stirred themselves for any ordinary householder.

It is not too much of a stretch to place the story of Joseph b. Simai's fire in the context of what we have noted about the fire fighters of ancient Rome. The record shows that these firefighters usually served in the city of Rome itself, but some units of well-trained and professional fire fighters served at other locations in Italy. Thus it is possible that the troops (or perhaps a para-military unit, a distinction that would hardly interest the talmudic editor) who came down to put out the fire may have been a unit of Roman professional firemen posted to the Sepphoris military base. This is only a possibility, of course, but it is an interesting one, because it would then suggest that firefighters were sent to the eastern regions of the empire as well as the western regions, and rather early in imperial history at that.

At any rate it is quite clear that Joseph b. Simai refused the services of the firefighters (one can imagine their incredulity at this Jew's strange behavior), but he obviously soothed any ruffled feelings with handsome gratuities for all hands. Joseph apparently knew how to keep his Roman friends happy.

The *baraita* on b.Šabb. 121a and its parallels present the first stage of the law on Sabbath fire fighting. The matter is perceived only as a serious violation of the Sabbath, unless human life is in mortal danger. There is no attempt to examine the implications of an "endangered" life, and no indication that anyone grasped the idea that a fire which may at first destroy only property will, probably sooner than later, endanger lives as well, when the fire is out of control and has become more than the people can effectively handle.

SECOND STAGE OF THE LAW

The second stage of the law on Sabbath fire fighting reflects some advance beyond the strict ancient view. This second stage is articulated in thirteenth-century Germany, and comes from R. Mordecai b. Hillel, the younger contemporary and pupil of R. Meir of Rothenburg. It is a technical discussion of Sabbath fire fighting, but not apparently a responsum dealing with a specific set of facts (Mordecai to tractate *Šabbat*, no. 393). The text begins with the observation that the Babylonian Talmud implies that rescue on the Sabbath is allowed, but not the extinguishing of flames. Even according to R. Simeon, who holds that a person who performs "work," which is not in and of itself "necessary work" on the Sabbath, is not liable thereby for the violation of the Sabbath (the violation involves *useful* work); and the prohibition with respect to such unnecessary work is a rabbinical prohibition, protecting Sabbath rest. Even here, writes

Mordecai, we do not set aside a rabbinical prohibition in order to effect rescue (of property). The Palestinian Talmud explains the basic text in this matter as following R. Judah, who held that extinguishing fire is a transgression of a biblically based law; one is also *held liable* for a transgression with respect to work *which is not necessary in and of itself.* According to R. Simeon, we may set aside a rabbinical prohibition only in order to rescue sacred Scriptures from a fire on the Sabbath. According to the Palestinian Talmud, however, this permission is limited to the rescue of sacred Scriptures, but it does not apply to other classes of property, even according to R. Simeon. Even though one may extinguish a fragment of red-hot metal on the Sabbath, *so that the public will not be endangered by it,* one has by so doing violated a rabbinical prohibition (see *b.Šabb.* 42a). The violation is permitted because there is concern for physical injury just as one may put a bowl over a scorpion that it not bite. But the loss of property alone is no permission to extinguish fire on the Sabbath.

The language and the context of public safety are evident in the passage, but that path is not traveled. Public safety does not become a prime consideration. Mordecai continues:

> In many lands it has now become the practice to extinguish fire on the Sabbath. They [who do permit this] have nothing on which to base [themselves in the legal tradition]. They say, however, that [they do this because] they are apprehensive that young children who cannot flee the blaze will die in the fire. Further, there is the fear of possible danger to life, because of the ill-will of the civil authorities and the non-Jewish population if they see us leaving the fire to burn unchecked. Therefore, they fight fire according to the view of R. Simeon. This is not a clear basis of permissibility, however. This is rather like what the talmudic sages said:"Leave the Jewish people alone [that is, let them do what they are doing although it is unlawful]; it is better they sin in error than by a wanton and calculated disregard for the law."

One might paraphrase the opinion as, what they do not know will not hurt them.

The first stage of the law was reflected in the versions of the talmudic anecdotes about R. Ammi and Joseph b. Simai. In that stage fire fighting on the Sabbath was permissible, indeed demanded, only if the fire endangered a life. The Mordecai text reflects a different view of matters that grows from the popular awareness that "danger to life" may include the risk of harm from non-Jews if the Jews simply let the fire burn on a Sabbath. They are also concerned for young children who might be too terrified or too confused to flee the danger. (The same may be said of the ill and elderly.) Both these ideas, or popular justifications, suggest that a fire which originally had threatened only property may become ever more dangerous to property and to life if it is simply allowed to burn. The concept of *piquah nefesh,* saving a life from mortal danger, now includes more than imminent danger from flame. The non-Jews were certainly not interested in the fine points of Jewish law when the flames were rising on a Sabbath and threatening their property; a fire unchecked poses a serious danger to people of all ages and backgrounds no matter what day of the week it starts. R. Meir in a responsum (ed. Prague, no. 140) calls attention to the vicious practice of throwing a Jew into the flames of his own house if the fire started in it. This was certainly enough to make Sabbath fire fighters out of the Jews or at least some of them — the householder in R. Meir's case fled the scene to escape danger.

R. Mordecai thought the halakhic justification, that the effort is permissible according to R. Simeon's opinion, was weak and certainly unconvincing for him. It is really no halakhic justification at all as is clear from the first part of the comment: only holy Scriptures may be rescued. The people have on a practical level, however, opted for "good public policy" justifying it as best they could. We have moved from a strict attitude of "let it burn" as long as no lives are in danger. In the older, stricter attitude, the danger appears to be understood only as the danger of the flames themselves. This attitude also countenanced turning away the help of non-Jews to fight the fire, or alternatively, asserting in the hearing of the non-Jews the neutral statement: he will be at no disadvantage (for fighting the fire — and perhaps he will be remunerated for the effort?). But apparently rabbinic opinion, which is clearly aware of an expanded version of "danger to life," thus implicitly acknowledges the idea that a fire left unfought will become a danger to life in more ways than one. Rabbinic authority, however, still appears very reluctant to grant permission to fight fire on the Sabbath. The people should be left alone, hands off, since it is better that they sin in ignorance than wantonly break the law. That is as far as the Rabbis would apparently go.

THIRD STAGE OF THE LAW

The third stage is the crucial turning point in the development of this modality of perception. This stage comes in the fifteenth century, roughly 200 years after the Mordecai's comment and the notations that non-Jewish mobs had no compunction about throwing a Jew into his burning building if he were not fighting the fire! The authority who authored this further development is R. Israel Isserlein of Wiener-Neustadt, whom we met earlier deciding a case of battery, although there is no indication that he saw himself as a genuine innovator in this matter of fire fighting.

Professor Shlomo Eidelberg, in his study of Jewish life in Austria in the fifteenth century, based largely on the writings of R. Isserlein, refers to texts which

he claims show the state of opinion on firefighting on the Sabbath and allude
to the Jewish law on the subject. Prof. Eidelberg[3] writes that fire was a communal problem for both Jews and non-Jews. The public safety concern raised
by fire, no matter where or when it started, therefore transcended any paro-
chial consideration. Fire did not care what was in its path. Death and destruction were indiscriminate.

Professor Eidelberg cites *Terumat Hadeshen* extensively, both the sections of
Responsa and *Pesaqim U'Ketavim*, R. Isserlein's, and the *Leqet Yosher*, written by
Isserlein's devoted pupil R. Joseph Moses (Joslein), as sources for a number of
statements about Jews and firefighting on the Sabbath. Between the two, we
have a glimpse into this phase of Jewish life in Austria in the fifteenth century,
but unfortunately those sources do not really support some of the assertions
Prof. Eidelberg makes with respect to firefighting.

Prof. Eidelberg, for instance, writes that when a fire broke out, both Jews and
non-Jews rushed to the fire scene to extinguish it. He cites *Pesaqim U'Ketavim*
55, 60, 158, and *Leqet Yosher* I:62, which parallels *Pesaqim U'Ketavim* 156. Those
texts simply address the matter of fighting fire on the Sabbath when serious violations of Sabbath rest would result from any fire fighting efforts. The text only
asserts an unqualified permission for Jews to pitch in and fight the fire since,
according to *Pesaqim U'Ketavim* 156, if Jews do not help out, the non-Jews
might kill them, or at least plunder their property. Matters had apparently not
changed much in that regard since the days of R. Meir and R. Mordecai b. Hillel.
But no one is described as rushing to extinguish the fire.

The permission to fight fire was, however, publicly preached. Prof. Eidelberg suggests that an address which the sources quote in part was delivered at
the time of the fire of 1406, which started in the Jewish quarter of Vienna on a
Friday night. The sermon was quite unequivocal. Both *Pesaqim U'Ketavim* 156
and *Leqet Yosher* I:62, 63, relate that R. Aaron Blumlein, R. Isserlein's uncle and
teacher, made it very clear that fighting a fire and doing one's share of the work
involved was a religious duty because danger to life was present. Such danger
overrides the rules on Sabbath rest. The texts also say that a rabbi who is asked
about such a matter is blameworthy because he had not already made clear to
his people that fire must be fought even on the Sabbath.

There is nothing in either text, however, that really supports the specific date of
1406, except for the comment in *Leqet Yosher* that the fire destroyed two-thirds
of the city, which the 1406 fire did. This comment about the two-thirds clearly
suggests the 1406 fire, and indeed that may be enough to establish a post-1406
date for the text in *Leqet Yosher*, a text which seeks guidance on the matter of

3 Shlomo Eidelberg, *Jewish Life in Austria in the XV Century* (Philadelphia: Dropsie College, 1962)
   pp. 35, 36 and the footnotes thereat.

the people who had excavated a vault on the Sabbath in order to protect their property, the problem we consider next.

Prof. Eidelberg refers to *Terumat Hadeshen Pesaqim U'Ketavim* 60, and *Leqet Yosher* I:62, 63, as reflecting methods of fire extinguishing at that time. This is incorrect. The texts refer to an underground vault (or a "cellar") that the Jews excavated in order to hide their valuables. They filled the holes with dirt up to the ground level, tamped it down and plastered stones and dirt together over the vault to protect its door, which was underground and made of wood, from fire. This entire procedure, which certainly took some time, was admittedly conducted on the Sabbath. In the confusion and alarm, they forgot it was the Sabbath. (Had they not been to synagogue?)

The rabbinic response to the question was entirely negative. These people had violated the Sabbath only for the purpose of securing their property; danger to life was in no way alleviated — indeed it may have increased. The non-Jews finding no ready plunder may well start killing Jews if they cannot carry off any loot. These passages also say nothing of fire fighting methods, unless the construction of the underground vault is taken in that light. The vault was obviously a means of protecting property, not fighting fire. In fact they suggest a negative picture: the Jews mentioned in responsum 60 seem to have worked furiously only to protect their valuables. They were doubtless too busy to fight the fire that threatened them and appeared to have had no thought for the danger of their neighbors.

Prof. Eidelberg also writes that a conviction for arson carried a death penalty, and that this was an added incentive for Jews to fight fire on the Sabbath. The same texts that were supposed to reflect modes of fire fighting are referenced for this assertion. The material, however, does not mention arson, or a conviction for arson, or a death penalty for such a conviction. Arson was indeed a capital offense in Roman law, which was doubtless the basis for the civil code in effect in R. Isserlein's time in the Austrian territories where he lived. *Pesaqim U'Ketavim* 156 and *Leqet Yosher* I:62, clearly do say that non-Jews are wont to throw a Jew into the flames of his own house when the fires started there. Isserlein notes that this is the same sort of violence that R. Meir of Rothenberg mentioned (and, for that matter, which R. Mordecai b. Hillel hints at as well). This is murderous brutality, not a conviction for arson. There is no element here of legal process, just the cruelty of going out to kill the Jew and to plunder what is available. The only trace of legal process at all, and it is only a trace, occurs in the responsum 58, the next text to be examined.

The fullest single statement on the question of fighting fire on the Sabbath is found in *Terumat Hadeshen* no. 58.[4] Although much of the same material

4 Israel Isserlein, *Responsa of R. Israel Isserlein*, sec. 1, *Terumath Hadeshen* (ed. Venice, 1519) no. 58.

appears in other parts of *Terumat Hadeshen, Pesaqim U'Ketavim* and *Leqet Yosher*, this responsum presents the more orderly and clearer statement. It omits only one element which will be noted at the end of the full rendering presented here (but not however word for word). Where the text cites another source, that source is reviewed in its own right; the source may not always be precisely as R. Isserlein cites it. The responsum is, however, substantially accurate in all its citations.

> *Question*: [Re:] A fire that has occurred on the Sabbath: Is it permissible for a Jew at this time to extinguish the fire or not [since the work involved clearly violates the Sabbath]?

> *Answer*: It would appear that there is a difference [of opinion] on this matter as I shall explain. The notes on *Hagahoth 'Asheri* to tractate ᶜ*Erubin* [4:6 re: p. 45a] based on '*Or Zarua*' to the fourth chapter of tractate ᶜ*Erubin* read as follows: At the present time if brigands come to plunder property [we] go out against them with arms and violate the Sabbath because of them. Similarly it is permissible to extinguish a fire at the present time because we live among non-Jews. When there is a fire, they come to plunder and to kill, [and this situation is] not of a lesser [degree of seriousness] than that of an Israelite town which stands in continuing danger from armed brigands [whom the Jewish residents may resist with armed force even on the Sabbath, compare *b.ᶜErub*. 45a].

This statement is identified as a citation from the '*Or Zarua*', the thirteenth-century compilation of R. Isaac b. Moses of Vienna. The most recent scholarly edition of this work says something rather different. In the section on the Laws of Sabbath Eve, 36:3, there is a brief discussion of R. Ammi's assertion that the rabbis permitted a person to say (in the presence of a non-Jew, in a Sabbath fire emergency) anyone who extinguishes the fire is not at a disadvantage, a provision which by now is very familiar. '*Or Zarua*', then makes several points:

As a practical matter of law '*Or Zarua*' writes that there is no differentiation between the work required for fire fighting as a Sabbath violation and other types of Sabbath violations. He adduces support for this opinion from *y.Šabb*. 15c. He suggests that if fire is comparable to armed incursion or flood, with respect to physically saving threatened property, how much more are they all comparable in the matter of permissibility merely to utter, (in the presence of a non-Jew) "anyone who saves . . . is not at any disadvantage," which is not physical activity but mere utterance (in any event not a sinful violation of the Sabbath: Jews are not responsible for a non-Jew's observances.) There is no reference to living among gentiles who come to plunder during a fire emergency, and so on, in section 36 or any adjacent section.

The citation of the notes on Rabbenu Asher is substantially accurate. The reason for fighting the fire is apparently to preclude a predatory raid that could cost Jewish lives as well as property, R. Isserlein continues to cite 'Or Zarua'.

In 'Or Zarua', Laws of Sabbath Eve (sec. 38) [the author] wrote as follows:

"Even in the case where there is only possible danger to life, even the great men of Israel extinguish the fire [on the Sabbath] even though it is possible for a non-Jew to do the work." (This is of course an echo of the talmudic dictum we have already noted.)

The next portion of the Isserlein responsum is not taken from 'Or Zarua'. Isserlein writes:"I have found that one of the great ones copied sermons of R. Haim 'Or Zarua' [the son of R. Isaac 'Or Zarua' to the following effect]: In a fire emergency in which there is danger, lest they should come to shed Jewish blood, do not tell a non-Jew to extinguish the fire. Rather it is a religious duty for the Jew to extinguish it himself.

"And one of the great ones preached publicly that it is permitted to extinguish a fire on the Sabbath at the present time; and he says that therefore he preached publicly that he not be termed negligent with respect to lives, as one says in this sort of matter, 'the person asked is ashamed' [if he delayed conveying his message:] he should already have made [the permissibility] public knowledge . . ."

The sense of this statement is made clear in R. Jacob b. Asher's *Tur 'Orah Haim* 328. When a person is ill and there is possible danger to life, one should not delay treating the patient, even if a Sabbath violation is involved, in order to ask whether such and such an act is permitted or not. In *y.Yoma* 8:45b, it says, "the one questioned is ashamed [to receive such an inquiry, the answer to which is so well-known] and the questioner is a murderer" (see also *Beth Yosef* to *Tur* 328 thereon). Isserlein continues,

I have heard [men suggest] unconvincing and awkward [arguments] to add greater strictness in this matter on the basis of their personal reasoning, saying, [the permission to fight fire applies] only when the fire first occurs in a Jewish dwelling. That is where the flames started. Because the non-Jewish rule was such: when they would find him [the Jew] from whose house the fire spread, they throw him into the fire.

This is the implication of the Mordecai to chapter eight of *Baba Meṣi‘a*ʾ, that thus was the non-Jewish rule (compare also Mordecai to *Baba Meṣi‘a*ʾ, 376). The word rendered here as a "rule" is the Hebrew "*mishpat*" which usually means judgment, or law, in this sort of context. The use of this word stretches its meaning to cover what appears to be a fairly common barbarity, a practice that Jews understood as tantamount to a "law." The word does not, however, appear in either the responsum of R. Meir of Rothenberg or the version of the responsum in the Mordecai. R. Isserlein himself (or perhaps R. Joseph b. Moses) interpolated it. In Isserlein's responsum 156 the same matter is described as "the way of the non-Jew." R. Isserlein continues:

> In this situation [where non-Jews would throw Jews into the fire] it is permitted to extinguish the fire. If, however, the fire began in a non-Jewish dwelling, one need not have this apprehension [about such immolation], and there is no danger. We have seen that [in] many major cities, in which large fires have occurred, [they — the non-Jews] did not harm the Jews physically at all. And not even a threat [of such brutality] was heard when the fire did not erupt in a Jewish dwelling. It seems, however, that on the basis of the language of the *Hagahoth 'Asheri*, there is no such implication that a distinction should be made according to the fire's place of origin, because the reason there [in the *Hagahoth 'Asheri*] depends on the proposition that, because they plunder and kill, [the situation] is not of a lesser [seriousness] than that of an Israelite town which is adjacent to the border. The implication of this language is that because one engages in the seizing of property, one may eventually engage in murder. By this reasoning one should be apprehensive about plunder and murder even when the fire originally spread from the dwelling of a non-Jew. They are always accustomed to pillage and plunder [and thus to murder] when the fire develops destructive power. Even if we observe that there are cities where no threat of this kind is ever heard of, one should not rely on that fact since on some few occasions, one does need to be apprehensive [of the possibility of plunder and murder], because the rule is established in chapter two of tractate *Yoma* [this citation is incorrect; the citation should be to chapter eight: *b.Yoma* 84b] that we do not follow a majority in matters where an immediate danger to life is concerned [*b.Ketub.* 15b].

That is, one searches through the rubble of a collapsed building on the Sabbath even though only one person in ten buried there might be a Jew. The text resumes:

> And just so do we find matters in *Tosafot* to *Niddah* 44a, s.v. *'ihu*, that we do violate the Sabbath even [to care] for a moribund person even though most such people do die. And [we] adduce proof for this from chapter two [that is, eight] of *Yoma*, as above.

The permission to fight a fire that begins on non-Jewish property clearly suggests that R. Isserlein understood that a fire left to rage would soon be a general threat to lives and property. The distinction between saving a life, even if only doubtfully in danger, and saving only property, is now really quite blurred.

R. Isserlein resumes:

> It would appear, however, that one should give careful consideration in any [specific] matter to the view of the [Jewish] sages of that city. For instance, if the civil authority in the city promises to rescue Jews [from depredations in, for example, a fire situation] and in this wise it seems that there is no danger at all, they should not violate the Sabbath at all [by fighting the fire or rescuing property contrary to the rules of Sabbath rest, but they certainly would save lives].

This is a somewhat obscure statement. Granted that the non-Jewish civil authority would be quite able to protect Jews from mobs of looters if a fire occurred in the Jewish area, there would still be the danger to life and property from the fire itself. On should not imagine that the civil authority could call out a fire brigade to fight fire in the Jewish neighborhood while the Jews merely stood by. Firefighting in R. Isserlein's era was primitive and rather unorganized at best, and if the Jews would not have lifted a finger to help fight such a common threat, the non-Jews would simply turn their attention to protecting themselves. R. Isserlein goes on,

> The language of R. Haim [noted] above implies that there are times when there is no danger, since it is written, "In a fire emergency in which there is danger lest they should come to shed [Jewish] blood," which intimates that without further information [to the contrary] we do not argue [or conclude, decide] that there is danger.

That is, the phrasing "a fire emergency in which there is danger to Jewish lives" also bespeaks a circumstance in which there is no such danger. When that is the case, one need not reason that there is in fact danger to Jewish lives and property without good reason to do so.

But how trustworthy would past assurances of safety really be in the fear and confusion of a fire that is out of control? There are two problems. First, control of the fire, and second, the control of mob looting and violence. Without some effective means of fighting the fire, looting is an excellent possibility, perhaps an inevitability. Even with the best of intentions, it may still be doubted whether or not any civil authority can absolutely control elements who are bent on plunder and murder. R. Isserlein suggests that such a serious matter as Sabbath violation be left to the competent rabbinic authority on the scene. Even here, however, one is hard put to imagine how a court would have time to convene, deliberate and decide while the flames grow higher in the absence of firefighters.

R. Isserlein's opinion also appears in *Beth Yosef* to *Tur 'Orah Haim* 334. *Beth Yosef* repeats the *'Or Zarua'* material, the *Hagahoth 'Asheri'* and much of the substance of the Isserlein responsum. R. Moses Isserles in *Darkhe Moshe* to *Tur 'Orah Haim* 334 cites more of the *'Or Zarua'* noting, among other things, that any permission to extinguish a fire on the Sabbath is only for the purpose of saving lives, but to desecrate the Sabbath for the purpose of saving property alone is still forbidden.

R. Isserles includes the Isserlein responsum in his gloss to *Shulhan 'Arukh 'Orah Haim* 334:26, mentioning *'Or Zarua'* and the notes on *Hagahoth 'Asheri* with their respective opinions. He concludes by saying that fighting the fire is only permissible on the Sabbath when lives are at stake, not just property. Further, if a person did transgress the Sabbath by fighting fire to save property alone, he must fast for forty days, on Mondays and Thursdays (therein), drink no wine and eat no meat (Sabbath and festivals excepted); he must also give a prescribed amount of charity. He may choose to "redeem" the fast and obviate its observance by giving a fixed amount to charity for each day of the fast (compare *Darkhe Moshe* to *Beth Yosef* on *'Orah Haim* 334). *'Or Zarua'* had also discussed fasting; he mentioned a practice of encouraging men to fight fire on the Sabbath *and then imposing the fasting regimen on them for the Sabbath violation preformed for a good and worthy cause* (*'Or Zarua'* Laws of Sabbath Eve, sec. 38). He does not, happily, accept this approach as a practical procedure. He holds that one should not do anything that might make men reluctant to fight fires in the future. This latter idea is most important in the fourth stage of this law's development, which we shall presently encounter.

The matter of fasting is not mentioned in responsum 58, but Isserlein does raise the matter in *Pesaqim U'Ketavim* 55 and 60 (see also *Leqet Yosher* I:63) where it seems the atonement in question there applies to types of work that were clearly transgressions of biblical rules.

The Isserlein responsum 58 (and the summary of it in *Shulhan 'Arukh 'Orah Haim*) expresses the third stage of development of the law on Sabbath firefighting. This third stage asserts that there is indeed justification in the Jewish tradition for Jews to become firefighters on the Sabbath. Saving lives is a religious duty, and the expanded definition of what constitutes danger to life is fully accepted. The danger may be from hostile mobs who will kill the Jew on whose property the fire started — or who declined to fight the fire, because it was a desecration of the Sabbath. A pragmatic public safety point of view becomes the accepted view. Danger need not be only from the flames per se. Authorities now appear to understand that unless the Jews take a hand in firefighting, even on the holy Sabbath, not only might they not expect any aid from non-Jewish neighbors or authorities, but they may well have to face mob violence for their extreme piety, apparently a sad fact of German-Jewish life for a long time. Fighting fire when lives are at stake directly or indirectly, so it appears, is now lauded as a classic religious duty. But fasting may still be necessary.

The Isserles gloss is a summation of the state of the law up to the close of the sixteenth century. But the gloss does not tell us what actually happened at times of emergency. Possibly, as we gather from 'Or Zarua', R. Meir of Rothenburg and Mordecai, that Jews had as a matter of fact fought fires on the Sabbath; others, as one might gather from the story of the underground "vault," took measures to protect their property rather than fight the common danger. Presumably "firefighters" who saved only property humbly accepted whatever fasting and penitential requirements were laid upon them. That is the most charitable presumption; yet they might also have disclaimed to do so, asserting that they had done a great public service and had saved lives. We do not know whether or not matters were really resolved that way. There are no responsa that reflect any such decisions in an actual case.

The one Jewish legal element that still acts as a possible barrier to full permissibility for Sabbath firefighting is this matter of a transgression of the Sabbath which, even if performed for a good and worthy cause, still requires expiation. This is clear in the major texts on the matter up to the end of the sixteenth century: 'Or Zarua', R. Isserlein, R. Isserles. The tradition holds that even if the danger to life is perhaps doubtful – is it or is it not a genuine danger – the fire may be fought and no fast or other expiation is called for. But should it be quite clear that the firefighting saved only property, and lives were never really in danger, the expiation is in order.

FOURTH STAGE OF THE LAW

The fourth stage concludes the long slow progression, from the bare permission to save a life endangered on the Sabbath and the willingness to let the fire burn if only property were involved, to this last stage which is a comprehensive public safety stance, that in effect protected both lives and property. The responsum that demonstrates the fourth stage appeared about a century after the career of R. Isserles. Someone finally asked the vital question about sin and expiation with respect to fighting fire on the Sabbath.

The seventeenth-century German authority R. Ya'ir Haim Bacharach speaks to the matter of desecration of the Sabbath by firefighting to save only property.[5] His response to the question shines a light on a matter that none of the previous authorities had really analyzed. Here is the question he was asked to resolve:

> You asked me about the matter of profanation of the Sabbath committed by reason of a fire [doubtless firefighting and fire rescue from the nature of the answer]: Is it proper [in that circumstance] to decree a public fast, because it was a sin of the congregation [apparently many men of the community

---

5   Ya'ir Haim Bacharach, *Hawwoth Ya'ir* (ed. Lemberg, 1894) sec. I, no. 236.

took part?] Certainly [this fire-fighting effort on the Sabbath] is a duty; there is no question about that [when life is in danger]. You are aware of the [opinions] of *Hagahoth 'Asheri* to *'Eruvin,* chap. 4 and R. Israel Isserlein *Terumath Hadeshen,* no. 58, and *Pesaqim U'Ketavim,* no. 60, which hold that there is no prohibition [against such activity] at all. On the contrary, a person diligent in this work is praiseworthy.

If your question concerns a profanation of the Sabbath in order to save property when there was no danger at all to life, the plain truth of the matter is that atonement is necessary [for so doing].

This is also made clear in the *Pesaqim U'Ketavim,* no. 60, cited above as well as in the gloss to *Shulhan 'Arukh, 'Orah Haim,* 334. R. Bacharach restates the law as R. Isserles and his predecessors put it: rescue of property alone entails expiation. Presently he will take a much closer look at the transgression. He goes on,

If it is your sense of the matter that there [remains] some apprehension that [some aspect of] a prohibition [is still involved here], because even though the situation concerned saving life, the saving of property was also effected by extinguishing the fire; this matter does not require careful examination, because there is *no* apprehension [that there is some transgression when property is saved in the process of saving a life]. [This is clear from] *b.Yoma* 84b [where a person saved a drowning child by catching it in a fish net, a worthy and proper act was performed] even though fish were also caught in the process.

Your wish may be [to receive guidance in the matter of] a mere stringency [of the law], because we find that there can be a religious duty, the performance of which requires expiation [compare *t.Ta'an.* 11a s.v. *'amar . . .*], and similarly in the *gemara* of *b.Sanh.* 26b, end, "they responded that they had performed a religious duty [yet they had to make an expiation].

This is the same ground that '*Or Zarua*' traversed centuries before, and it requires a closer inspection. In this *Sanhedrin* citation, some gravediggers had buried a corpse on the first day of the Feast of Weeks, an act which was both a meritorious act and a desecration of the festival. One rabbi excommunicated them as wicked men. Another rabbi lifted the excommunication: the gravediggers may have reasoned that they did indeed transgress, and the time spent in excommunication was the penance the rabbis imposed on them. The parallel to the act of fire fighting as a "meritorious transgression" is clear. R. Bacharach continues:

In *b.Mo'ed Qat.* 9a the expression, "All the goodness shown to the people Israel" [2 Kgs 8:66] indicates to the Rabbis that the sin of non-observance of the day of Atonement had been graciously forgiven the people." [What the text contemplates is this: the Solomonic Temple was being dedicated. The dedication ceremonies fell at the time of the Day of Atonement, ordinarily a day of pious introspection and fasting, quite out of harmony with the joy of the dedicatory events. The people, therefore, did not observe the Day of Atonement that year, a sin punishable by extirpation (*karet*) see Lev 23:29, 30].

The text resumes:

> Even though the Rabbis employed an *a fortiori* argument to allow the sacrifices of the individuals to be offered at the Temple, and an *a fortiori* argument has the force of a biblical provision, one gathers [nonetheless] that pardon was necessary [that is, they had been pardoned for the non-observance of the Day of Atonement, yet it was still necessary to seek forgiveness].

The argument *a fortiori* is intricate. What the respondent contemplates is a complex matter of sacrificial ritual. In the case of the desert Tabernacle, whose sanctity was not eternal, *individual* sacrificial gifts were offered at the time of its dedication even on the Sabbath day. Ordinarily the offering of *individual* sacrifices on the Sabbath is a capital offense. The Solomonic Temple, whose sanctity is eternal, was celebrated at its dedication with "public" offerings that ordinary people, not just priests, could eat; and these were offered even on the Day of Atonement, the desecration of which is punishable by extirpation (*karet*), a lesser degree of punishment than capital punishment. Thus, if the individual gifts were allowed at the dedication of the Tabernacle and the imposition of the capital punishment (that is, the more severe penalty) did not apply *a fortiori*, how much the more were the public offerings (which were eaten on that fast day) permissible at the Temple on the Day of Atonement during the Temple's dedicatory celebration (compare Lev 23:29, 30), a matter calling for extirpation, *karet*, the lesser level of punishment. The rabbis take the verse in 2 Kings to mean that the people were forgiven the sin of the non-observance of the Day of Atonement, and yet expiation and forgiveness were still necessary. That was of course a special exception for the dedication; there obviously could be no such permanent permissibility.

The text resumes:

> We find a disagreement along these lines concerning uncleanness caused by a corpse [with respect to the High Priest on the Day of Atonement who must be absolutely ritually pure]: is such uncleanness, if contracted, rendered permitted [that is, rescinded so that the High Priest may offer public sacrifices] or is it only suspended?" [In the matter under notice, is the

sin of desecration of the Sabbath by reason of firefighting erased entirely
or is it merely "suspended," and thus pardon is necessary?]

The responsum continues:

> The *Bet Yosef* to *Tur 'Orah Haim* chap. 328 examines the matter of saving
> life on the Sabbath along these lines ["permission or only suspension"],
> and concludes that the Sabbath is [only] *suspended for the purpose of sav-*
> *ing a life*. If so, [that is, if this reasoning is correct] it appears that there is
> a [valid] line of reasoning that expiation is required [*for saving the life on*
> *the Sabbath* — there was only a *suspension,* not a cancellation, of the strict
> law of Sabbath observance].
>
> Thus, to my humble way of thinking, wherever the Rabbis have said:
> Great is the honor due to humankind for it suspends a negative command-
> ment of Scripture [*b.Ber.* 19b *et passim*], expiation is required. I say that,
> with respect to profanation of the Sabbath [because of an acceptable rea-
> son], granted it is good and proper for the individual to fast, that it not be
> only a matter of choice [for him to do so]: R. Huna once got the strap of his
> *tifillin* somehow reversed, and he fasted forty days [because of it] [*b.Moʿed*
> *Qaṭ.* 25a]; and *b.Ḥag.* 22b [relates the story that R. Joshua] was ashamed [for
> having spoken somewhat harshly of Shammai, the great sage of genera-
> tions before]; and R. Joshua's teeth were black from fasting. [The point of
> these anecdotes is that rabbis undertook to fast for even the most minor
> lapses in ritual or etiquette . . .] In any event, since we have seen that our
> Sages of blessed memory were very sensitive about this matter of saving
> a life [on the Sabbath, by means of a Sabbath violation]. And [they said]
> we do not do these things [save lives] by using women or slaves [to do so]
> [*b.Yoma* 84b], to which R. Nissim [fourteenth-century Spain, Rabbenu Nis-
> sim to Alfasi *Yoma* 4b, at *W'ein*] commented: so that people would not say
> that they gave the permission [to save a life on the Sabbath] only with dif-
> ficulty [that is, this permission to save a life by violating the Sabbath was
> only allowed despairingly, in disappointment, and permitted only as a last
> resort so to speak]. How much the more [would this last notion appear
> correct] if they were to decree a public fast for saving a life by transgress-
> ing the Sabbath — because one should be apprehensive lest [by so doing]
> you would cause [potential rescuers] to stumble in the future: that people
> would refrain and not perform [rescues], because they would stop fight-
> ing fires on the Sabbath!

Even though this argument was clearly on the record for a long time (*'Or Za-*
rua' had made it), R. Isserlein did not include it in his presentations of his legal opinion nor did R. Bacharach. Therefore, one has to assume that the fourth

stage did not fully emerge until the seventeenth century. As far as I can tell, no major authority has reopened the matter since as a live issue. The text resumes:

> Therefore, one should not instruct in this wise [to require the rescuer who violated the Sabbath to fast etc.] and all the more not to decree a public fast. And the one who is more stringent [in this, by requiring a fast] is [really] being lenient; he is a person who causes others to wonder at his strange behavior! [He thinks he is being strict, but really he gives people an excuse to shirk a clear duty.]
>
> How much the more should there not be any fasting imposed if one's "profanation" is not a type of work forbidden by Scripture, but [merely] the moving of fire fighting implements [this is the only reasonable meaning of k'lei s'refah] and the like. How much the more [is there no violation worthy of fasting] if he has only given them [the implements] to the water-drawers, and he gives [them] to his non-Jewish colleague [in this work] and that one to another one [and so on down the line], because there is [in this] only the most minor violation of Sabbath rest, and it requires no repentance at all.
>
> So it appears to me, Yair Haim Bacharach.

R. Bacharach has cleverly eliminated virtually the last explicit element of difficulty in the way of a complete public safety and public order perspective. He could not simply erase the matter of fasting, but he does the next best thing. He minimizes the transgression involved in firefighting on the Sabbath until it all but vanishes. The process runs like this: Since the weight of tradition has clearly dismissed the necessity for expiation where there is a life threatening situation or even a possible threat to life, the only profanation still in question concerns a profanation for the sake of saving property alone. R. Bacharach begins by reasserting the necessity for expiation for this sort of transgression although he is surely aware that the distinction between a life-threatening fire and a fire endangering only property is too rigid to maintain in practice, a point which is implicit in the justification of firefighting when there is *possible* danger to life. Second, the expiatory regimen, therefore, applies only where mere property is at stake. Third, R. Bacharach finally devalues the actual act of profanation: working the bucket brigade, the probable meaning of moving the "implements"; that is, helping to fight the fire, is only a *minor violation of Sabbath rest.* Expiation is thus an unnecessary burden to place on firefighters, lest they become reluctant to answer the call in the future. Therefore, since the distinction between a life threatening emergency and a non-life threatening emergency in an urban setting is all but impossible to maintain, the minor infraction that would occur in the latter case is no cause for expiation. There was always danger to life from fire in the sorts of urban settings where Jews lived. As long as there was a potential for some life saving effort, a religious duty was involved and atonement and expiation are no longer a problem. R. Bacharach has deftly all but removed the matter of atonement and expiation from the "violation" of Sabbath firefighting.

There is conceivably still a problem with actually throwing water on a fire. That is more than merely passing water buckets to the scene of the blaze. But it would be extremely difficult to prove that throwing water on a fire was *only* for the purpose of saving property. The point is always well taken that any fire may easily become a possible mortal danger. R. Bacharach has for all intents and purposes achieved a view of firefighting that accords entirely with the perspective of public safety. The forth stage has finally been achieved.

To review briefly: the first stage is the most rigid, characterized by Joseph b. Simai's refusal of non-Jewish aid and the rule that the most one may do is to inform a non-Jew somehow that if he fights the fire he will be at no disadvantage. Fire is to be fought only if a human being is endangered by it, that is, by the flames; if property is also saved, this is acceptable under the law. The first stage emphasizes the seriousness of violating the Sabbath. The second stage acknowledges an implicit expansion of the idea of "danger to life"; yet there is reluctance to approve the arguments that some Jews used to justify what they in fact did. The third stage is approval of Sabbath firefighting to save endangered lives, however those lives may be endangered by the fire; directly by flames or indirectly through mob violence, plunder and murder at the time of fire emergency. There is also a reiteration of the ancient talmudic principle that to engage in saving a life from destruction is a religious duty incumbent upon all Jews. Yet there remains the problem of performing a religious duty by breaking a religious prohibition against saving mere property, in order indirectly to prevent loss of life. In this situation, the violation, though in this case excused, may still require atonement and forgiveness. The final stage implicitly rejects the necessity for fasting and expiation – in virtually every case. Participation in the bucket brigade of firefighters involves only the most minor sort of infraction, and fire is in practical terms always a danger to life. If the firefighters' efforts could be proven to be wholly a matter of saving property, then the expiatory regimen might possibly apply but that would be extremely difficult to prove, assuming someone would care to raise the point as a practical matter. Further, if the firemen who (as it turned out) saved only property had to fast, would they continue to fight fires that might occur on the Sabbath? Arguably some sorts of firefighting tasks could still constitute a violation if the work involved were of a different nature: perhaps actually throwing the water on the fire to extinguish it; surely the actual extinguishing of flame might be deemed a more serious level of violation. Or perhaps destroying property to clear a fire break was a graver sin. No authority was called upon to analyze these matters.

We should, however, keep in mind that those acts would become violations of the Sabbath only if it were proven that the fire in fact threatened only property, a rather tall order. If the law has not moved through a 180-degree arc, it has moved at least 175 degrees in this four-stage process.

The "modality" here is a shift in perspective and a broader understanding of what fire danger involved. This rethinking provided a sound basis for maintaining public safety and the well-being of the community. R. Haim Benveniste, a Sefardi and an older contemporary of R. Bacharach, comes to the same conclusion as R. Bacharach in this matter.[6] R. Benveniste also records the rule on fasting and charitable giving stated by R. Isserles in his gloss noted above. R. Benveniste draws attention to R. Isserles's reference to permissibility of Sabbath firefighting even if there is only possible mortal danger to people. He then asserts that on the basis of this view, we now have permission to fight fires on the Sabbath in any circumstance. Obviously he subscribes to the idea that the fire will sooner or later represent possible danger to life. This permission he propounds applies whether or not there is danger from civil authorities (or a mob?) if the Jews do not fight the fire. The ill and the elderly will be endangered if the fire is unchecked.

Further, suggests R. Benveniste, most of the time, people's property is prey to plunder at the time of a fire emergency, and a person is much concerned for his goods. If he just rescues his property, the mob will kill him. R. Benveniste concludes his comment with the remark that in his view it is not proper to make the permissibility of firefighting on the Sabbath well known. On one hand, he acknowledges that Sabbath firefighting is permissible. But on the other he is ultimately reluctant to make this a matter of public knowledge. We recall that in the time of R. Isserlein, R. Blumlein passionately urged Jews to fight the Sabbath fire. The permission to fight the fire on the Sabbath arguably becomes the standard approach, and R. Bacharach disposes of the need to fast and atone for it. The only question is whether this permissibility shall become well known in Jewish communities, a matter that R. Bacharach did not raise and very likely would have answered in the positive, contrary to R. Benveniste.

Even though the two men were contemporaries, no reason exists to believe that they knew of each other's work. Certainly R. Benveniste was dead long before R. Bacharach's work appeared and R. Bacharach does not mention R. Benveniste's conclusion which would have strengthened his own halakhic opinion. He could have either omitted R. Benveniste's problem with publicity in the matter, or reasoned it away on the basis of R. Isserlein or *Leqet Yosher*. After all, the permission itself was not in doubt, only its publicity.

The *halakhah* shifted, very slowly but very surely, from the rigidity of the

6 Haim Benveniste, *Kenesseth Hagedolah* (ed. Leghorn, 1657) to *'Orah Haim* 334, Beth Yosef, no. 11.

ancient talmudic discussions, that looked on Sabbath firefighting as a purely ritual matter, to the public policy view that took the realities of life very much into account. Reluctance and refusal to act should one reason that property alone was at stake were eventually superseded by the necessity to do what had to be done when fires occurred. Rabbinic authorities of the most impeccable orthodoxy adapted the law to the demands of life.

Rabbinic authority from the thirteenth century explicitly states that Jews indeed did fight fires on the Sabbath. 'Or Zarua', R. Meir of Rothenburg and the Mordecai all make that quite clear. Undoubtedly they fought fires on other days of the week as well. But one finds no sources that actually describe Jews on the fire line except perhaps for R. Bacharach's likely reference to a bucket brigade. That reference, however, may merely be describing something R. Bacharach has seen, that may or may not have involved Jews at all. But that is not the entire story. Some Jews obviously fled for their lives, terrified that an angry mob might pitch them into the flames of their own houses. Some saw to their property first (perhaps later joining the firefighters?). People react to the danger of fire in different ways, and the material we do have suggests the range of such reactions. The clear tone of strong encouragement and support for the firefighting in the fifteenth-century sermon cited in R. Isserlein's responsum may reflect a reluctance on the part of at least some of the community to get involved with it. Some people seemed to have needed powerful persuading that it was the right thing to do. What is clear is that at no time did fire prevention or fire fighting become a Jewish communal enterprise. It remained a matter of individuals who stepped up when the occasion demanded. Although saving lives was and is a major desideratum in Jewish law, the task of doing so rested on individuals as individuals. No general public duty seems to have emerged, but the conclusion that fire fighting is licit on any day of the week is a modality for the enhancement of public order and safety, which preserves the lives of individuals, whether menaced directly or indirectly.

Conclusion

The leadership of the various medieval Jewish communities, including Rabbis, rabbinic courts and lay courts, superintended the maintenance of public order and public safety within their bailiwicks. It could not have been a pleasant duty since it meant confronting lawbreakers, possible lawbreakers and all manner of persons and situations that disturbed the public peace or held the Jewish community up to ridicule and derision, or to destruction, as in a fire, or both. But this was as important a task of leadership as the maintenance of religious, educational and charitable institutions which themselves surely required a more or less safe and orderly society in which to function.

The communities applied various modalities for the preservation and maintenance of public safety and order. In Spain, where some communities possessed royal sanctions to impose capital and corporal punishments, these penalties appear to have been imposed — or at the very least approved — by rabbinic authority. Even where such measures were not available to Jews, Jewish leadership was no less forthright in handing down penalties commensurate with the seriousness of the offense.

The Jewish courts in effect took such measures as they deemed necessary. Although some of the measures were traceable to talmudic practices, what we have is a system dictated both by the limits of Jewish law and the independent judgments of rabbis and other communal leaders. The ancient doctrine of "special measures to meet the necessity of the hour" required individuals of unimpeachable piety and honor to decide what had to be done in the various medieval cases. The courts chose among fines, which were technically unlawful under strict talmudic law, floggings, excommunications, injunctions, public humiliations, preventive incarcerations, and procedures for the reconciliation of parties to arrive at what the leadership believed to be the proper resolution to a breach of public peace and public order. And they at length found a reasoned basis for what amounted to the general permissibility of firefighting, a genuine area of public safety. The communities were creative in these quests. The law was a supple tool in the hands of men, special men to be sure, but men nonetheless. It is altogether reasonable to see what they did as subject to the rule of men just as much as it was to the rule of law.

This inquiry has exposed some of the less exalted or inspiring episodes of medieval Jewish history. Some of what was done, or was proposed to be done, was cruel and inhuman by modern standards. Some of it does not rise to a modern standard of legality, but the medieval world did not run according to our rules, and necessity overrode moral idealism from time to time even among the most sensitive, learned and pious of our ancestors. The rabbis well understood that they were to pursue justice, but justice was justice for the greater good of the people as a whole, not necessarily for the individual. Doubtless we would not often do as they did. Yet they are by no means to be faulted or derogated for their defense of their standards of public order, safety, and, indeed, decency. This concluding thought is much the same as the idea expressed when we began this inquiry. We have come full circle through the modalities for the maintenance of public order and safety in Medieval Jewish law.

Appendix 1
A Plea for Calm

The record discloses a situation in which a Rabbi could take no really positive steps to restore order when a serious incident involving homicide apparently polarized a community. R. Haim b. Isaac *Or Zarua*, son of the illustrious compiler of *Or Zarura*, pupil of R. Meir of Rothenburg and contemporary of the *Rosh,* faced just such a situation.[1] One group of Jews drew knives and swords against another group of Jews and chased them out of a banquet. We do not know what prompted the violent behavior. The ejected party apparently complained to a non-Jewish court. One suspects fines were imposed on the attackers. In the course of events they also *perhaps* secured the service of an apostate Jew who led gentile assassins to the home of the leader of the rival group. The assassins killed that man. R. Haim decides that the Jewish law on homicide simply did not apply in this matter, except to the person (perhaps an apostate Jew) who actually brought the killers into the house. Further there is no liability for any economic loss the relatives of the deceased caused their assailants through action of the non-Jewish court.

The decision amounts to a declaration that no one has a case under Jewish law. What the Rabbi really wants is an end to the rancor and tumult. None of that will bring the dead back to life. The matter could go on endlessly and that would certainly not be in the best interest of the peace and good order of the Jewish community. The Rabbi outlines no steps for conciliation or reconciliation. That was doubtless too much to ask in such a heated atmosphere. He simply wants an end to the public quarrel. There was no room for family strife after the fashion of the Montagues and the Capulets in the medieval Jewish community.

---

1 Haim b. Isaac, *Responsa of R. Haim b. Isaac "Or Zarua'"* (Leipzig: K. W. Wollrath, 1860) no. 25.

Appendix 2
The "Arresting Officer"

In the review of the classic rules, I alluded to the fact that no person or persons was charged with the duty of bringing an accused wrongdoer before the court.[1] There are, however, references both in the Talmud and in post-talmudic material to various individuals whose duties may have included the task of finding and presenting offenders before the court.

R. Elazar b. Simon was appointed a "thief taker" for the Roman government, a role which did not endear him to his fellows since such a person necessarily had to have close contact with the underworld and in the course of his duties had to deliver co-religionists to a brutal Roman justice.[2] He was in a sense an informer, and bore opprobrium because of his informing. Since he worked for the government, he was not presumably in awe of any penalties an informer faced under the *halakhah*. No doubt there were other thief takers as well, but their names and exploits are not recorded.

Then there was the *shilah bet din*, the agent or emissary of the rabbinical court. He is not identified as an "arresting officer," though his duties may have included such an office. Further, the agent of the court does not appear to have been a regular appointee, at least none of the discussions of the compositions of medieval courts seems to mention such a regular officer. He was probably an *ad hoc* appointee: required to perform a particular service which probably included the serving of summons, delivery of divorce documents, and perhaps arrest. He is also noted as one who wielded the whip in floggings. We do have a responsum from the late seventeenth or early eighteenth century which recounts a severe thrashing the emissary of the court administered to an individual right in the courtroom.[3] It is not clear at all in the case that the victim of the *shaliah*'s anger was the accused or some person who indeed struck the officer.

The agent of the court enjoyed a degree of immunity for damages he caused to property in the course of his duties; and his statements to the court within the scope of his duties also enjoyed protection.[4] Indeed the agents may have from time to time been arresting officers. The court could designate a person as an agent on an as-needed basis.

1 See above, p. 16.
2 *b. B. Meṣ.* 83b.
3 Jacob Reischer, *Shevuth Ya'akov* (ed. Halle, 1710) 180. See also S. M. Passamaneck, "The Use of Excessive Force by a Peace Officer," *Jewish Law Association Studies* 1 (1985).
4 Isserles's gloss to *Shuḥan Arukh Hoshen Mishpat* 8:5 summarizes the officer's immunities. The Karo text simply says that one is prohibited from acting improperly towards him or to cause him difficulty in the performance of his duty.

The Jewish courts, particularly in Spain, apparently could call upon non-Jewish assistance, perhaps in the matter of arrest, or coercion. The *Rosh* alludes to just such a procedure.[5] Neuman describes the courts as exercising a public power that was quite broad, but interestingly there is no mention of a police officer as such, much less an arresting officer for public safety and public order.[6]

Finally we have come to the term *shoter* (pl. *shotrim*), the modern Hebrew noun for police officer. Although the word appears in tannaitic sources, it really is not clear what these public officers did. Indeed they may have had powers of arrest yet one really cannot assert that such was the case. Maimonides was not at all hesitant about the matter: for him the *shotrim* were market inspectors, who were armed and had the duty to bring wrongdoers to court; presumably they could haul any wrongdoer they caught before the magistrate, not just persons with faulty weights and measures.[7] The term *shoter* in medieval rabbinic material also denoted non-Jewish officials, governmental officers who surely had powers of arrest.[8]

Obviously in some cases a victim could come to court and accuse a person of, for example, theft or battery and demand that he be held to answer the charges. He might summon members of his family to assist him or the court might appoint burly fellows to bring him in. The simple fact is that we really do not know how the medieval court went about the process of arrest. What we can say with certainty is that they did contrive by some means, probably a variety of means, to bring the accused to court. Whether a court had a person or persons they regularly called on for the purpose, and whether they called him an agent of the court or something else, really makes no difference in the long run. Such persons left few and indistinct traces on the record. The requirements of public order and public safety demanded that the accused be brought before the court. Somehow this was done; the details are unimportant. Public order and public safety could not be protected unless someone preformed the task of "arresting officer."

5 *Responsa of R. Asher b. Yehiel*, 6:27.
6 Neuman, *The Jews in Spain*, vol. 1, chap. 7, particularly p. 144. Police power indeed, but no mention of specific police officers.
7 *Mishneh Torah Hilkhot Shofetim* 1:1. Maimonides is, of course, describing a justice system for a reconstituted Jewish state. His description of the *shoter* may or may not have had any real relation to past reality or his contemporary world.
8 See Stephen M. Passamaneck, "The *Shoter*," *Jewish Law Association Studies* 12 (2002).

Excursus
Human Rights and *Kavod Habriut*

Surely various of the modalities we have examined abrade if not downright brutalize, modern western sensibilities. They are medieval with all the agony and horror which that adjective can suggest. We have duly noted that the rabbinic authorities mentioned were perfectly aware of the humane and decent aspects of Jewish tradition. That can not be denied. Yet the only clear echo of "humanity" is the demand that the handless cripple be provided some means of livelihood. There is no hint of mitigation of the harshness of the prescribed penalties. Indeed, one text asserts that the judge who imposes sentence and then finds whatever grounds he might to soften the blow is acting improperly.

Where then do we find the concern for humanity that modern Jews often hold to be at the heart of Jewish tradition? Where is the concern in these matters for what we term today human rights?

Let us first distinguish between civil rights and human rights. The state confers civil rights upon its citizens (and non-citizens if it so chooses). Human rights belong to the human being simply by virtue of his or her humanity. The framers of the United States Constitution held that such rights are an endowment from the divine, and in just such wise have human rights often been considered for over 200 years.[1] They are not granted from one person to another, one does not earn them; they spring whole from one's humanity itself: among them, Life, Liberty, and the Pursuit of Happiness.

Jewish tradition certainly holds Life and Liberty dear. Pursuit of Happiness need not detain us.[2] Human life takes precedence, at least in theory, over every other consideration except willful homicide, some gross sexual offenses noted in Scripture, and idolatry. The human being is created in the image of the divine, and Jews are not to destroy that image.[3] Liberty is another clearly held value. The festival of Passover — the festival of Freedom — proclaims the central role human freedom occupies in Jewish values. Life and Liberty stand close to the heart of the list of values to which many modern Jews subscribe. They are often held as crucial. Other values — charity, peace, learning, kindness — all flourish in the rich soil of Life and Liberty.

---

1 The Universal Declaration of Human Rights passed by the General Assembly of the United Nations, December 10, 1948, does not mention the role of the divine in Human Rights which the Preamble to the United States Constitution 1787–89 does. The Declaration consists of a Preamble and 30 Articles.

2 Happiness, it may be argued, is only definable in terms of individual perception; what is happiness for person A may not be so for person B. Jewish tradition knows of many sorts of happiness and supports them all unless they involve some offense or moral lapse or both.

3 Gen 1:26, 27.

The question then becomes whether or not, when human rights are couched in the language of Jewish tradition, we are really hearing a true echo of the tradition itself or we are hearing grand humanist ideals from seventeenth- and eighteenth-century philosophy rephrased to harmonize with Judaism and imported as though they were original within the tradition. Do these human rights spring from our millennial tradition, which often reflects an exalted moral sense in any event, or from other sources which have been lovingly incorporated into the catalog of Jewish values?

The late Prof. Haim Cohn wrote an extensive examination of human rights and Jewish law.[4] He clearly asserts that no concept of human rights as we know them today appears in Jewish law.[5] Rather the mainspring of Jewish jurisprudence is a complex system of duties, commandments, revealed by the divine and incumbent upon Jews to the greatest extent possible. One may suggest, as Cohn does, that duties imply some sort of right; for instance, the duty not to murder may imply a right to life and the duty to aid the poor may imply a right to some nominal livelihood.[6] Yet it is equally valid to avoid the notion of rights and hold that such duties imposed on an individual are at bottom a service to God: one is not to destroy people who are in the divine image or allow them to suffer from want and privation for to do so is a gross offense to God who will exact condign punishment. There need be no necessary reference to the "right" of a person to life, liberty, or property. The person is incidental to the duty to obey divine law: do not murder; help the poor. Although a "right" to property may be inferred, it is just as reasonable to infer a capacity to own or possess property rather than a "right" to it. One has the capacity to hold property as long as one can maintain possession and control of it. No one is permitted to interfere with this holding of property; but it is not really a "right," much less an enforceable right.

Do we have here a distinction without a difference? Does not the system of duties, by implication at least, bespeak the existence of something akin to "human rights" in Jewish tradition? I think not. In the modern world human rights are explicitly stated. They are not left to inference or implication. Further, Jewish law, as a revealed tradition (at least in theory), imposes duties which foremost serve God and, incidentally (but no less importantly) humanity. The focus is always on the service of God. Divine honor is never to be compromised.[7]

---

4 Haim H. Cohn, *Human Rights in Jewish Law* (New York: KTAV, 1984) particularly the first chapter. Prof. Cohn was also a Justice of the Israel Supreme Court.

5 Cohn, *Human Rights*, 18, 19.

6 Cohn, *Human Rights*, 18, 19.

7 One may, in theory at least, break any law, except those against murder, incest-adultery involving a Jewish married woman, and idolatry, in order to save one's life. But the story is more complicated than that; see Stephen M. Passamaneck, "The Jewish Mandate or Martyrdom," *HUCA* 74 (2003) 215–41.

While Judaism finds much that is wonderful in the concept of human rights that appeal arguably reflects moral sensitivity and a commitment to ethical living rather than some classic theme of Jewish law as such. One certainly cannot assert a human right against the divine. The idea of human rights is part of the western philosophical tradition of the Enlightenment, which Jews gladly accepted upon their emancipation from medieval thrall. Jewish legal tradition tends to reinforce the maintenance of human rights through the specific duties incumbent upon Jews, but the rights themselves as a program of civilized morality did not emerge as an expression of Jewish tradition per se. It is one thing to assert a program of human rights which flow from the fact of humanity itself. It is quite another to claim that they are embedded in commandments and service to the divine; they may or may not be so embedded, and they need not be inferred from it.

Suffice it to say that Jewish tradition has its own mode of recognizing, supporting and enhancing human dignity and seconding the assertion of human rights. Yet we have clearly seen that the Rabbis and community leaders of the Jewish past never allowed such considerations to sway them when the peace and order of their societies were endangered: capital punishment, corporal punishment, incarceration and even some forms of torture, were all legitimate modalities for a court with sufficient authority and power to impose. In Cohen's discussion of cruel punishments and torture, there is no reference to these medieval cases. He deals only with the classic rules, the exercise in exoneration.[8]

The Hebrew phrase *kavod habriot* is occasionally suggested as a Hebrew formulation of the notion of human rights. The phrase however means something more like the respect due to humanity. It has no overtone of any "right" enforceable or not. In its talmudic contexts, and it is indeed an ancient expression, the phrase suggests a modicum of modesty in personal matters or in the treatment of a corpse.

The expression appears in a most interesting talmudic discussion which at first glance appears to clothe the concept of human dignity with great significance.[9] The *gemara* asserts, "Great is human dignity since it overrides a negative commandment of Scripture." This suggests that human dignity, indeed human rights, were held in high esteem. The text explains, however, that the negative command in question is a very specific one: ". . . Thou shalt not turn aside [from the ruling they shall declare to you]" (Deut 17:11). Human dignity may override this particular negative commandment, not negative commandments as such. The Gemara clarifies the matter thus: this particular commandment is the basis for rabbinical enactments. You shall not turn aside therefore means

8 Cohn, *Human Rights*, 217–24, 225–29.
9 The relevant text is *b.Menaḥ.* 38a.

that a person shall not disregard the rulings of the rabbis; the statement does not refer to biblical commandments. Where human dignity is involved, however, as in matters of personal hygiene or dress, a rabbinic enactment may be set aside. There is not, therefore, any clarion to raise human dignity as a basis for any broader non-observance of commandments. Moreover, the Talmud does not perceive *kavod habriot* in any broad sense. It is not a rabbinic paraphrase of human rights. The expression continues to bear its rather narrow meaning throughout both talmudic material and post-talmudic commentary.

Had the Rabbis, ancient or medieval, wished to expand the notion into a grand general principle of law, or for that matter, of ethics and morality, they surely could have done so. Here was an opportunity to elevate the notion into something akin to the present-day idea of human rights. But they did not do so. Only when Jews awakened to a new world in which the Rights of Man had captured the imagination of men and nations in the Western World did they search for such an idea within their own tradition.

Finally, the expression *kavod ha'adam*, the "respect" or "dignity" due a human being, another possible Hebrew formulation for "human rights," rarely appears in rabbinic literature.[10] There is no occurrence of it in any context involving public safety or public order. The modern term for "rights," *zechuyot*, which also suggests merits, privileges, or benefits, does not occur at all in medieval rabbinic literature. This does not detract from nor diminish the significance of its its modern meaning. The Rabbis of old, however, simply did not recognize it or employ it.

---

10 The Bar Ilan database yields only four instances of the phrase.

Bibliography

Just as the area of public order and public safety has been largely overlooked in Jewish law, so too the bibliography for it is correspondingly small. The bibliography provided here notes only those works, particularly responsa, which do deal with problems touching such matters and of course some secondary literature, to the extent that it bears upon the subject. Standard works such as the Mishnah, the Babylonian and Palestinan *Talmudim*, the *Arba'a Turim*, the *Shulhan Arukh* and the like are not included. The numerous citations to those works are easily found in any of their standard editions that include a full apparatus of commentary, for example, *Mordecai*, or *Ha'gahot Asheri*. The references to those standard halakhic works obviously imply their use and further bibliographic notation is really superfluous.

Agus, Irving. *Rabbi Meir of Rothenburg.* Philadelphia: Dropsie College, 1947.

Asher b. Yehiel. *Responsa of Asher b. Yehiel.* Venice: Alvise Bragadini, 1552. New York: Grossman, 1954.

Ya'ir Haim Bacharach. *Hawwoth Ya'ir.* Ed. Lemberg, 1894.

Baer, Yitzhak. *A History of the Jews in Christian Spain.* Trans. Louis Schoffman. 2 vols.; Philadelphia: Jewish Publication Society of America, 1961–66.

Haim Benveniste. *Kenesseth Hagedolah.* Ed. Leghorn, 1657.

Ben Menahem, Hanina and Neil Hecht. *Selected Topics in Jewish Law.* 2nd ed.; Boston: Institute of Jewish Law, 1988. Vol. 2.

Berkowitz, Beth A. *Execution and Invention.* Oxford: Oxford University Press, 2006.

Cohn, Haim H. *Human Rights in Jewish Law.* New York: KTAV, 1984.

Shimon b. Zemah Duran. *Responsa of R. Shimon b. Zemah Duran.* Ed. Amsterdam, 1738–39.

Eidelberg, Shlomo. *Jewish Life in Austria in the XV Century.* Philadelphia: Dropsie College, 1962.

Epstein, Isidore. *The Responsa of R. Solomon b. Adret.* New York: KTAV, 1968.

Finkelstein, Louis. *Jewish Self-Government in the Middle Ages.* New York: Feldman Publishing Co., 1964.

Freehof, Solomon. *The Responsa Literature.* Philadelphia: The Jewish Publication Society of America, 1955.

Haim b. Isaac. *Responsa of R. Haim b. Isaac "Or Zarua."* Leipzig: K. W. Wollrath, 1860.

Hershman, Abraham. *Rabbi Isaac b. Sheshet Perfet and His Times.* New York: Jewish Theological Seminary of America, 1943.

Isaac b. Sheshet Perfet. *Responsa of Rabbi Isaac b. Sheshet Perfet.* Ed. Constantinople, 1546.

Israel Isserlein. *Responsa of R. Israel Isserlein*, sec. 1, *She'elot U'teshuvot*, and
sec. 2, *Pesaqim U'Ketabim*. Ed. Venice, 1519.

Israel b. Haim of Bruenn. *Responsa of Israel b. Haim of Bruenn*. Ed. Salonika,
1798.

Judah b. Asher. *Responsa Zichron Yehudah*. Berlin: Friedlander 1846; repr.;
Jerusalem: n.p., 1967.

Kapah, Joseph. *Responsa of R. Yom Tov b. Abraham Ashbili*. Jerusalem:
Mossad Harav Kuk, 1958.

Kirschenbaum, Aaron. *Introduction to Jewish Law*. Herzliah: Interdisciplinary
Center, 2005.

———. *Self-Incrimination in Jewish Law*. New York: The Burning Bush Press,
1970.

Lewin, Benjamin M. *Otzar Hageonim, Bava Qamma*. Jerusalem: Mossad
Harav Kuk, 1943.

Neusner, Jacob. *A History of the Jews in Babylonia: 2, The Early Sasanian
Period*. StPB 11. Leiden: Brill, 1966.

Passamaneck, Stephen M. "The Use of Excessive Force by a Police Officer."
Jewish Law Association Studies 1, 1985.

———. "The Berure Averot and the Administration of Justice in XIII and
XIV Century Spain." *Jewish Law Association Studies* 4, 1990.

———. "R. Judah b. Asher on Capital Punishment," *Jewish Law Association
Studies* 7, 1994.

———. "Remarks on Pesquisa in Medieval Jewish Legal Procedure." *Jewish
Law Association Studies* 9, 1996.

———. "Ancient Traces of Investigative Profiling." *Jewish Law Association
Studies* 10, 2000.

———. "The *Shoter*." *Jewish Law Association Studies* 12, 2002.

———. "The Jewish Mandate of Martyrdom." *HUCA* 74, 2003.

———. "Biblical Arsonists and Sabbath Firemen." *Mellilah*, 2005.
http://www.mucjs.org/MELILAH/2005/2.pdf, Nov. 25, 2008.

Quint, Emanuel and Neil S. Hecht. *Jewish Jurisprudence*. 2 vols.; London,
Paris: Harwood Academic Publishers, 1980–86.

Rakover, Nachum. *Multi-Language Bibliography of Jewish Law*. Jerusalem:
Library of Jewish Law, 1990.

Jacob Reischer. *Responsa Shevuth Ya'akov*. Ed. Halle, 1710.

Solomon b. Adret. *Responsa of R. Solomon b. Adret*. 7 vols.; Tel Aviv: Sifriyati,
1957–65.

Jacob b. Judah Weil. *Responsa of Jacob Weil*. Jerusalem: Safra, 1959.